Culture
and International Business

Culture and International Business has been co-published simultaneously as *Journal of Transnational Management Development,* Volume 4, Numbers 3/4 1999.

The *Journal of Transnational Management Development* Monographic "Separates"

Below is a list of "separates," which in serials librarianship means a special issue simultaneously published as a special journal issue or double-issue *and* as a "separate" hardbound monograph. (This is a format which we also call a "DocuSerial.")

"Separates" are published because specialized libraries or professionals may wish to purchase a specific thematic issue by itself in a format which can be separately cataloged and shelved, as opposed to purchasing the journal on an on-going basis. Faculty members may also more easily consider a "separate" for classroom adoption.

"Separates" are carefully classified separately with the major book jobbers so that the journal tie-in can be noted on new book order slips to avoid duplicate purchasing.

You may wish to visit Haworth's website at . . .

http://www.haworthpressinc.com

. . . to search our online catalog for complete tables of contents of these separates and related publications.

You may also call 1-800-HAWORTH (outside US/Canada: 607-722-5857), or Fax 1-800-895-0582 (outside US/Canada: 607-771-0012), or e-mail at:

getinfo@haworthpressinc.com

Culture and International Business, edited by Kip Becker, PhD (Vol. 4, No. 3/4, 1999). *Explores how many costly errors have been made by international businesses that have not realized the extent to which the needs and behaviors of consumers and employees vary among regions and nations.*

Globalization and Regionalization: Strategies, Policies, and Economic Environments, edited by Jean-Louis Mucchielli, PhD, Peter J. Buckley, PhD, and Victor V. Cordell, PhD (Vol. 3, No. 2/3/4, 1998). *"Goes a long way in clearly and cogently elaborating several arguments and perspectives that help us derive a thorough understanding of these phenomena." (Gopal Iyer, PhD, Baruch College, The City University of New York)*

International Business Education Development, edited by Zafar U. Ahmed (Vol. 2, No. 1, 1996). *Offers suggestions for program development or enhancement and stresses the importance of educating business school students with a global perspective.*

International Business Teaching, edited by Erdener Kaynak, PhD, DSc (Vol. 1, No. 4, 1996). *The tool for international business educators to meet the challenge and opportunity to graduate globally conversant and competent managers.*

Culture
and International Business

Kip Becker, PhD
Editor

Culture and International Business has been co-published simultaneously as *Journal of Transnational Management Development*, Volume 4, Numbers 3/4 1999.

International Business Press
An Imprint of
The Haworth Press, Inc.
New York • London • Oxford

Published by

International Business Press®, 10 Alice Street, Binghamton, NY 13904-1580 USA

International Business Press® is an imprint of The Haworth Press, Inc., 10 Alice Street, Binghamton, NY 13904-1580 USA.

Culture and International Business has been co-published simultaneously as *Journal of Transnational Management Development*, Volume 4, Numbers 3/4 1999.

The development, preparation, and publication of this work has been undertaken with great care. However, the publisher, employees, editors, and agents of The Haworth Press and all imprints of The Haworth Press, Inc., including The Haworth Medical Press® and Pharmaceutical Products Press®, are not responsible for any errors contained herein or for consequences that may ensue from use of materials or information contained in this work. Opinions expressed by the author(s) are not necessarily those of The Haworth Press, Inc.

The Haworth Press, Inc., 10 Alice Street, Binghamton, NY 13904-1580, USA

Cover design by Thomas J. Mayshock Jr.

Library of Congress Cataloging-in-Publication Data

Culture and international business/Kip Becker, editor.
      p. cm.
      "Culture and international business has been co-published simultaneously as Journal of transnational management development, volume 4, numbers 3/4 1999."
      Includes bibliographical references and index.
      ISBN 0-7890-0969-2 (alk. paper)–ISBN 0-7890-0987-0 (pbk.: alk. paper)
      1. International business enterprises–Management. 2. Management–Cross-cultural studies. 3. Intercultural communications. 4. Corporate culture–Cross-cultural studies. I. Becker, Kip.
HD62.4 .C854 1999
658'.049–dc21
                                                                                    99-057752

INDEXING & ABSTRACTING

Contributions to this publication are selectively indexed or abstracted in print, electronic, online, or CD-ROM version(s) of the reference tools and information services listed below. This list is current as of the copyright date of this publication. See the end of this section for additional notes.

- *Abstracts on Rural Development in the Tropics (RURAL)*

- *BUBL Information Service: An Internet-based information service for the UK higher education community <URL:http://bubl.ac.uk>*

- *Cambridge Scientific Abstracts*

- *Central Library & Documentation Bureau*

- *CNPIEC Reference Guide: Chinese National Directory of Foreign Periodicals*

- *EconLit, on CD-ROM, and e-JEL*

- *Foods Adlibra*

- *GEO Abstracts (GEO Abstracts/GEOBASE)*

- *Management & Marketing Abstracts*

- *Operations Research/Management Science*

- *Referativnyi Zhurnal (Abstracts Journal of the All-Russian Institute of Scientific and Technical Information)*

- *Sociological Abstracts (SA)*

- *Social Services Abstracts*

- *Work Related Abstracts*

(continued)

Special Bibliographic Notes related to special journal issues (separates) and indexing/abstracting:

- indexing/abstracting services in this list will also cover material in any "separate" that is co-published simultaneously with Haworth's special thematic journal issue or DocuSerial. Indexing/abstracting usually covers material at the article/chapter level.
- monographic co-editions are intended for either non-subscribers or libraries which intend to purchase a second copy for their circulating collections.
- monographic co-editions are reported to all jobbers/wholesalers/approval plans. The source journal is listed as the "series" to assist the prevention of duplicate purchasing in the same manner utilized for books-in-series.
- to facilitate user/access services all indexing/abstracting services are encouraged to utilize the co-indexing entry note indicated at the bottom of the first page of each article/chapter/contribution.
- this is intended to assist a library user of any reference tool (whether print, electronic, online, or CD-ROM) to locate the monographic version if the library has purchased this version but not a subscription to the source journal.
- individual articles/chapters in any Haworth publication are also available through the Haworth Document Delivery Service (HDDS).

Culture and International Business

CONTENTS

ABOUT THE EDITOR

Kip Becker, PhD, is presently an Associate Professor and the Chairman of the Department of Administrative Sciences at Boston University. He has published numerous articles and book chapters both nationally and internationally in the areas of international management, strategy, marketing and global service sector issues. He is the editor of the *Journal of Transnational Management Development* and on the editorial review boards of *Marketing, The Journal of Yugoslav Marketing Association, the Journal of Marketing Channels* and *the Journal of Teaching in International Business.* Dr. Becker is the Chairman of the Board of the International Management Development Association. He co-owns a waterfront restaurant and is president of Northwind Management International which has conducted management training and consulting with governments and companies worldwide. Prior to entering academe, Dr. Becker's experience included positions with TDX systems of Cable and Wireless Ltd., the U.S. Department of Justice and as a helicopter pilot with the U.S. Army.

Preface

Culture and International Business is a book devoted to the effects of culture on international business operations. Many costly errors have been made by international businesses that have not realized the extent to which the needs and behaviors of consumers and employees vary among regions and nations. Change has created many conflicts between the established ways and the introduction of new ideas and different behaviors. Even the oldest of cultures have found themselves susceptible to the forces of change. In 1994 Beijing, for example, got a Hard Rock Café and while accepting some of the Hard Rock Café concepts, Chinese censors did check the songs of the guest performer, blues legend B.B. King, for "political correctness." The advent of satellite television and inexpensive world travel has promoted a blending of cultures but has not lessened their distinct importance. As firms further their internationalization efforts more and more employees will find that they are being exposed to greater cultural diversity. This is true not only for those who travel among a company's locations but for those who have never traveled for the firm as well. This is increasingly the case due to efforts to expand hiring of indigenous persons to staff "foreign" locations. Often new managers from foreign subsidiaries are provided training in the domestic offices exposing not only them, but also those around them, to different ways of thinking. This internationalization of the workplace has placed increased pressures on human resource departments, managers and staff. As such, companies will find it increasingly difficult to respond to differing languages, values and perceptions in a manner that maximizes diverse personal qualities and achieves company goals. As Internet use, international

[Haworth co-indexing entry note]: "Preface." Becker, Kip. Co-published simultaneously in *Journal of Transnational Management Development* (International Business Press, an imprint of The Haworth Press, Inc.) Vol. 4, No. 3/4, 1999, pp. xiii-xv; and: *Culture and International Business* (ed: Kip Becker) International Business Press, an imprint of The Haworth Press, Inc., 2000, pp. xi-xiii. Single or multiple copies of this article are available for a fee from The Haworth Document Delivery Service [1-800-342-9678, 9:00 a.m. - 5:00 p.m. (EST). E-mail address: getinfo@haworthpressinc.com].

xi

travel and communication speed all increase it is certainly reasonable to assume that the velocity at which cultures collide will increase as well.

The seven articles included represent a wide range of issues and several geographic areas. The lead article by Kamal Dean Parhizgar discusses the evolutionary perspectives of multicultural management systems and their relationship to cultural, ethical and legal environments. The article co-authored by Madeline Crocitto and Maali Ashamalla uses a social theory framework to analyze expatriate-patriate relationships and proposes that employees of a host nation can be used to facilitate the expatriation process and stress that patriates are normally an underutilized resource that can offer valuable input into international human resource decisions.

Zhen Xiong Chen and Jiing-Lih Farh provide a review of 308 Chinese firms and compare the human resource management practices of township and village enterprises in relation to Sino-foreign joint ventures. Their findings are consistent with the predictions of institutional theory and provide further insights into the importance of cultural influences in management practices. Veronica Horton and Brenda Richey, in their article "Sampling and Selection Bias in International Collaborative Alliance Research: Is It Clouding Our Vision?" argue that an understanding of international alliances is limited by selection bias. Their discussion focuses on the belief that firms are strongly influenced by their headquarters' nationality and, as a result, companies have yet to have evolved as global citizens with global organizational styles. In "Determinants of Defender-Prospector Strategic Preferences: Examining the Effects of Personality and Culture," Steve Williams and Sunitha Narendran review the dynamic issue of strategy formulation and how individual characteristics direct and focus strategic choice decisions. In the article by Bater et al. the authors particularly note the importance of developing an interactive and adaptive approach which incorporates cultural factors when sustainable development strategies are designed by multinational teams. Hong Liu and Yen Po Wang's article demonstrates directly the importance of appreciating different cultural environments in international business transactions. Their study of 103 foreign partners from Sino-foreign joint ventures in China revealed that different relationship patterns between channel members significantly affected the ability of one channel member to affect the behavior of another. It was noted that behavior that was consistent with the domestic actions of firms had the potential of disrupting foreign channel member relationships. Chinese channel relationships require nurturing and the investment of time to develop. As such, it was shown to be fairly easy to develop an adversary relationship when stepping outside Chinese cultural boundaries.

It is interesting to note that the seven articles included in this volume were submitted by authors representing five different nations and three continents. The *Journal of Transnational Management Development* continues to be sincerely dedicated to encouraging global perspectives and research from OECD, developing and non-OECD nations alike. The editor and editorial board acknowledge that a certain degree of flexibility is necessary if this goal is to be realized as not all nations share similarly in resources or knowledge.

Kip Becker

Globalization
of Multicultural Management

Kamal Dean Parhizgar

SUMMARY. Based on a literature review of intellectual contributions by philosophers, scientists, researchers and scholars, this article illuminates the evolutionary perspectives of multicultural management systems. It bears in mind that international management practices reflect the societies within which business organizations exist. It is suggested that multiculturalism, which focuses on meritorious values of organizational incumbents, is an appropriate framework for international organizations. Many studies found evidence that multinational corporations in demographically diverse environments are more likely to emphasize over assimilation of cultural, ethical and legal value systems and that values proposed for international corporations to emphasize on similarities rather than differences. *[Article copies available for a fee from The Haworth Document Delivery Service: 1-800-342-9678. E-mail address: getinfo@ haworthpressinc.com <Website: http://www.haworthpressinc.com>]*

INTRODUCTION

The technological innovations, demographic movements, political events, and economic forces have changed over time and are continuing to change human behavior in the future. In today's increasingly

Kamal Dean Parhizgar is Professor of Management, Department of Management, College of Business Administration and the Graduate School of International Trade and Business Administration, Texas A&M International University, 5201 University Boulevard, Laredo, TX 78041-1999.

[Haworth co-indexing entry note]: "Globalization of Multicultural Management." Parhizgar, Kamal Dean. Co-published simultaneously in *Journal of Transnational Management Development* (International Business Press, an imprint of The Haworth Press, Inc.) Vol. 4, No. 3/4, 1999, pp. 1-23; and: *Culture and International Business* (ed: Kip Becker) International Business Press, an imprint of The Haworth Press, Inc., 2000, pp. 1-23. Single or multiple copies of this article are available for a fee from The Haworth Document Delivery Service [1-800-342-9678, 9:00 a.m. - 5:00 p.m. (EST). E-mail address: getinfo@haworthpressinc.com].

competitive and demanding international free market economy, managers can't succeed solely on their domestic cultural understanding skills alone. Chen and Eastman (1997: 454) indicate: "Despite differences in the level of analysis and standpoints of organizations versus subgroup, both the integration and differentiation perspectives on organizational culture are inadequate to address cultural conflicts associated with demographic diversity."

The purpose of this article is to present three dimensional views as a testable theoretical framework for conceptualizing multicultural management systems on the basis of heterogeneity rather than homogeneity. These three conceptual views are cultural, ethical and legal values in the multinational management systems. In the theoretical section, this article lays the groundwork for the integration of cultural, ethical and legal ideas in the international business transactions. Then, it illustrates how multicultural management systems can not be subsumed under either the "integration" or "differentiation" (Martin, 1993).

THE IDENTITY OF MULTICULTURALISM

In our contemporary international free market economy, multiculturalism can have a profound impact on peoples' lives. International business transactions are emerging from multi-functional, multi-disciplines, and multi-contacts among home and host nations. Nations come into frequent contact with what Gudykunst (1994: 4) would call "strangers"; namely, "people who are not members of our groups and who are different" on the basis of culture, ethics, legal, ethnicity, gender, or other group characteristics.

Technological development of today's business transactions among nations through the borderless information systems such as the World Wide Web (WWW) brought all nations together. Nations can't segregate themselves from the rest of the world. In addition, demographic movements among nations have provided new opportunities to assimilate different cultures, races, genders, age groups, and religions into a new form of international understanding–namely multiculturalism. These movements also provided two forms of identities: organizational and individual. Organizational identity is based upon the meritorious distinction among the division of labor, training, specialization, skills, and hierarchy of authority, while individual identity is illustrating different races, ethnicities, education, religions, colors, and others that all organizational members are striving to achieve collectively an organizational goal. The end result of such assimilation is called multiculturalism. For example, some researchers project that in ten years, ethnic minorities will make up 25% of the population in the United States. Copeland (1988: 52) asserts that: "Two thirds of all global migration is into the United States, but this country is no longer a 'melting pot' where newcomers are eager to shed their own cultural heritages and become a homogenized American." In the United States in the 1990s roughly 45 percent of all net additions to the labor force are non-European people (half of them first generation immigrants, mostly from Asian and Latin countries), and almost two-thirds are female (Cox, 1993: 1). These trends go beyond the United States. For example, 5 percent of the population of the Netherlands (de Vries, 1992) and 8-10 percent of the population in France are ethnic minorities (Horwitz and Forman, 1990). Moreover, the increases in representation of women in the workforce in the next decade will be greater in much of Europe–and in many of the developing nations–than it will be in the United States (Johnston, 1991: 115). Also, the workforce in many nations is becoming increasingly more diverse along such dimensions as gender, race, and ethnicity (Johnson and O'Mara 1992: 45; Fullerton, 1987: 19). For example, Miami-based Burger King Corporation recruits and hires many immigrants because newcomers to the U.S. often like to work in fast-food restaurants and retail operations. The reasons are:

1. flexible work hours (often around-the clock) allow people to hold two jobs or go to school,
2. Entry-level positions require little skill, and
3. High turnover allows individuals who have initiative and ambition to be promoted rapidly (Solomon, 1993: 58).

REVIEW OF THE LITERATURE

In a multicultural society like the United States, businesses thrive by finding common grounds across cultural and ethnic groups. But in homogeneous cultures such as European and/or Asian countries, businesses are maintaining their local value systems. While the entire concept and principles of management in all cultures are the same, the practice of management is different.

American people constantly change things–their images, homes, products, services, and the way they do things. To Americans, change is good; change is improvement. However, European and Asian cultures do not so easily discard their long and proud histories. They believe that patience and an established way of doing things are virtues, not weaknesses (Hill and Dulek, 1993: 51-52). Accordingly Americans believe that businesses that try to target each group separately will be stunted by prohibitive marketing costs. Others will meet this challenge by a multicultural consumer mix (Riche, 1991: 34).

From another dimension, in 1992, the European Union (EU) removed all tariffs, capital fund barriers, and people movement limitation among its member nations. It has created a potential trading block in the industrialized world and comprised at least 327 million people with different cultures and languages (Fernandez, 1991: 71).

The North American Free Trade Agreement (NAFTA) among the United States, Canada and Mexico has created another trading potential, some $212.5 billion annually, a base which should increase considerably (Gordon, 1993: 6). The Association of South East Asian Nations (ASEAN) is another organized intercontinental trading agreement among Brunei, Indonesia, Malaysia, the Philippines, Singapore, and Thailand to promote cooperation in many areas, including industry and trade. These and other intercontinental trade cooperations have changed the competitive international marketplace drastically.

In 1997 the total monetary value of all worldwide exports has been recorded by the International Financial Statistics (IMF) as $5,469.5 billion. Out of that sum, the developed nations exported $3,628.1 billion and the developing nations exported 1,841.4 billion (see Table 1-1). In the same year (1997) the developed nations imported $3,624.7 billion and the developing nations imported 1,989.9 billion (see Tables 1-2 and 1-3).

In the area of international business no conceptual approach pays as much explicit attention to the conceptual bases of thoughts and normative actions as multicultural evolution. We are witnessing the emergence of multicultural alliances that could rightly be called "global." This indicates that nations are more closed to each other and they need to establish a synergistic strategy to integrate the needs of all nations. As the United States has domestically shown a manifestation of the growth years, so did the incentive for companies to move branches of

TABLE # 1-1

TOTAL EXPORTS
In Billion $US

	1970	1975	1980	1985	1990	1995	1997
WORLD	298.4	844.0	1,921.8	1,849.4	3,377.6	5,079.1	5,469.5
DEVELOPED NATIONS	223.0	577.3	1,260.4	1,276.0	2,453.5	3,460.5	3,628.1
DEVELOPING NATIONS	75.3	266.7	661.4	573.3	924.0	1,618.5	1,841.4

Sources: International Finance Statistics (IMF), 1998.

TABLE 1-2

TOTAL IMPORTS
In Billion $US

	1970	1975	1980	1985	1990	1995	1997
WORLD	313.7	867.3	2,000.5	1,936.4	3,466.5	5,147.2	5,614.6
DEVELOPED NATIONS	223.5	603.9	1,400.3	1,347.2	2,573.2	3,412.9	3,624.7
DEVELOPING NATIONS	81.2	263.4	600.2	562.2	893.3	1,734.3	1,989.9

Sources: International Finance Statistics (IMF), 1998.

TABLE 1-3

TOTAL BALANCE OF PAYMENTS (BOP)
In Billion $US

	1970	1975	1980	1985	1990	1995	1997
WORLD	− 15.3	− 23.3	− 78.7	− 87.0	− 88.9	− 68.1	− 145.1
DEVELOPED NATIONS	− 9.4	− 26.6	− 139.9	− 98.2	− 119.6	47.6	3.4
DEVELOPING NATIONS	− 5.8	3.3	61.2	11.2	30.6	− 115.6	− 148.4

Sources: International Finance Statistics (IMF), 1998.

operation outside the home country in the form of strategic business subsidiaries (SBS). By the mid-1990s, companies based in the United States had nearly twenty thousand affiliates around the world (Jackson et al., 1997, 173). In addition, today more than 37,000 companies worldwide have foreign direct investments (FDI) that encompass every type of business function–extracting raw materials from the earth, growing crops, manufacturing products or components, selling outputs, rendering various commercial services, and so on. The 1992 value of these investments was about $2 trillion. The sales from investments were about $5.5 trillion, which was considerably greater that the $4 trillion value of the world's exports of products and services (World Investment Report 1993: 1-4). Considering the scope and magnitude of such international operations, the demand for multicultural understanding for more effective international collaboration is high.

The emergence of flowering multicultural communication began to take place as multinational corporations made a shift in their perspectives from solely domestic maximization of profitability to joint optimization of internationalization of individuals and organizational performances. Still, some political thinkers and business owners are generally prone to highlight the alienating influence of multiculturalism on their work-place. Marquardt and Engel (1993: 59) report that: "Based on the number of unsuccessful adjustments and early returns of American business expatriates, both government and private studies agree that more than 30 percent of U.S. corporate overseas assignments fail." Some corporate managers typically believe that for synergizing their corporate's wealth and maximizing their profit, it would necessitate institutions to exploit consumers and/or to sacrifice workers. However, the modern philosophy of multiculturalism rejects this view of either/or reasoning as a vision that under reciprocal justness, corporate workers' and consumers' satisfaction can synergize the corporate wealth and elevate their level of profitability. This belief is anchored in multicultural assumptions about all workers and organizations that power sharing and democratic processes facilitate corporate survival towards more profitability.

There are rational reasons by which multinational corporations should make an effort to apply multiculturalism in their organizations. Among the most important view is the fact that policies concerning the workplace and marketplace affect the quality of life styles, the economic well-being of working population, the enhancement of employees, and the synergistic technological innovations.

However, corporate managers must recognize that corporate opportunities are limited. They must also recognize that we do not live in an international meritocratic environment. They must recognize that multinational corporate bureaucracies are partially political. Operating in a competitive free market economy will not allow one to escape these realities. Corporate managers and workers of the multinational corporations must truly understand and effectively interact with other people from other cultures. They must understand both home and host countries' formal and informal values, rules, structures, norms, and attitudes of people and the real cultural criteria for solving social issues. For example, a multinational corporation which is operating in India, must recognize the traditional priorities of social castes of that country in terms of not appointing a manager from lower caste to supervise employees from the higher castes.

Specifically, cultural differences and status-determining criteria generally have quite different meanings in regard to time, place, and conditions culture by culture. In some *gerontocratic* cultures, the older persons are, the higher their status (e.g., France, Germany, Saudi Arabia, China, Russia and many other countries). However, in a *meritocratic* culture, once a person reaches a certain age, the status goes downhill.

CHANGING PROFILE
OF GLOBAL BUSINESS ENVIRONMENT

Anthropologists, sociologists, psychologists and economists have documented the fact that people in different cultures, as well as people within a specific culture, hold divergent value systems on particular issues. Bass et al. (1979) studied the attitudes and behaviors of corporate executives in twelve nations and found that our world is becoming more pluralistic and interdependent. Laurent (1983: 75-96) found in his research some differences across national boundaries on the nature of managerial role. Hofstede (1980a) corroborated and elaborated on the results of Laurent's and others' research results in a forty-country study, which was later expanded to over sixty countries (Hofstede, 1980b), in which 160,000 employees from American multinational corporations were surveyed twice. Hofstede, like Laurent, found highly significant differences in the behavior and attitudes of employees and managers from different countries who worked within multinational corporations. Also, Hofstede (1980a: 42-63) found that national culture explained more of the differences in work-related values and attitudes than did the position within the organization, profession, age, or gender.

Eitman and Stonehill (1979: 1-2) state that in the world today:

> Capital raised in London in the Eurodollar market by a Belgium-based corporation may finance the acquisition of machinery by a subsidiary located in Australia. A management team from French Renault may take over an American-built automotive complex in the Argentine. Clothing for dolls, sewn in Korea on Japanese supplied sewing machines according to U.S. specifications, may be shipped to Northern Mexico (Maquiladora plants) for assembly with other components into dolls being manufactured by a U.S. firm for sale in New York and London during Christmas season. A California manufactured air bus . . . is powered by British . . . engines, while a competing air bus . . . flies on Canadian wing assemblies. A Frenchman is appointed president of the U.S. domiciled IBM World Trade Corporation, while an American establishes . . . a Swiss-based international fund.

Multiculturalism is like snapshots taken from different angles and distances of societies at different times within the context of multinational organizations. No multicultural single picture or perspective as a multinational corporation can depict multifaceted character of human behavior, because diversified value systems differ in focus and scope of ethicality, morality, and legality (Harvey and Allard, 1995: 3).

No phenomena have fascinated researchers in the modern globalized and free market economy more than multicultural, moral and ethical value systems. In recent years, multinational management perceptions have been shaken. There has been much public concern. One belief is that the value systems of humanity that made the late twentieth century so achievable, are the results of global competitive cooperation. For example, American culture which represents multiculturalism is emphasizing on the importance of cooperation between workers and capital holders for more synergy. Some researchers concluded that there is a widespread ethical commitment among United States workers to improve productivity (Yankelovich, 1982: 5-8).

Another example is: what causes both employers and employees to strive for productivity? Do employees view work as a necessity of continuing their life? Is people's view on work a contractual binding between employee-employer commitment? Are they viewing work towards achieving higher levels of profitability? The answer to all these questions indicates that the more money a corporation gets, the harder they work, and the more profit they make the higher wages and benefits are paid to workers.

Profitability is a social contract, on the one hand, between workers and capital holders, and on the other hand it is a legitimate agreement between society and organizations, whose mandate and limits are set by ethical, moral and legal systems. The limits are often moral, but they also are frequently written into law. For example, in the early days of American enterprises, the Protestant work ethic was a strong influence, providing both motivation and justification for a business-person's activities. According to such an ethical value system, the good and hard working people were blessed with riches; the lazy and incompetent suffered (De George, 1995: 14).

The work ethics in multinational corporations have different dimensions. In some cultures, for example, ethics and morality have conceptual, technological, and legal aspects, while in others, they have social, ethical, and moral. The conceptual dimension consists of choosing among architectural scientific alternatives in designing and planning the operational processes of a business. The technological dimension consists of developing methods of embodying the new engineering and operational systems for producing new profitable products and processes. The legal aspect consists of discipline and order to govern the rightful use of wealth and power. In such cultures, workers' perception is essentially rational. Even in these cultures, workers believe that Mother Nature follows the laws of rational thoughts. Existentialists believe that thoughts and practicality abreast each other without overlapping. However, in other cultures, thoughts and rationality abreast each other in a dialectic reasoning and the results would be a synthesized conclusion in societal practicality.

However, Kirrane (1990: 53) indicates that: "The very term, 'business ethics,' tends to arouse some people's cynicism. They shake their heads and woefully recite recent scandals." Contrary to the beliefs that cultural and ethical value systems are just business buzzwords, they are often the major predictors of the success or failure in either an industry's or a company's strategy.

Within the globalized business environment, many people agree that some multinational corporations believe that their businesses should not be concerned with international philanthropy or with corporate ethics beyond their adherence to international legal requirements. The prominent business advisor Peter Drucker (1980: 190) has written that ethics is a matter for one's "private soul." Following his reasoning, he states that management's job is to make human strength productive. Further, economist Milton Friedman (1971) argues that the doctrine of social responsibility for businesses means acceptance of the socialist view, that political mechanisms, rather than market mechanisms, are appropriate ways to allocate resources to alternative uses. However, in globalization of international enterprises, altering people's cultural and ethical value systems is not the ultimate aim. Managing multicultural value systems among nations, is the challenging means to achieve successful globalization.

Many multinational corporations through various statements of beliefs communicate their organizational ethical, cultural, and legal value systems. These value systems have been called credos, missions or corporate philosophy statements. As Kirrane (1990: 56) indicates, Johnson & Johnson was surveying its employees for their views on the latest version of its corporate philosophy. Johnson & Johnson addressed its corporate beliefs about principal responsibility: "To doctors, nurses, patients, to mothers and all others who use our products and services globally, suppliers and distributors, employees, communities in which we live and work and to the world community, and stockholders." It concluded by saying that: "When we operate according to these principles, the stockholders should realize a fair return."

The problem facing executives, managers, and employees in globalizing corporations, is that few people within organizations comprehend all areas of organizational ethical, cultural, and legal systems in transition. As an example in Intel, senior managers usually concentrated on global strategy and structure. Middle managers complained that various aspects of the corporate culture prohibited them from acting globally. And human resource people focused on building better interpersonal and cross-cultural skills (Rhinesmith, 1991: 24-27).

Understanding corporate cultural, ethical, and legal value systems, in the time of conversion from domestic to global market operations, requires transition through several stages. Since members of international, multinational, and globalized organizations can enter with different cultural backgrounds and leave corporations very rapidly, managers try to leave corporate cultural and ethical value systems intact. However, alongside the globalization processes of a corporation, there are many issues which remain unresolved. For example, based on the promise that global strategy and structure can increase profits and promote growth, these concepts become the primary responsibilities of corporate managers. However, no consideration is given to cross-cultural relations between producers and consumers.

Today, some business school curricula have been designed to educate future business leaders on the basis of global *strategy* and *structure* in order to promote profit and growth. The curricula attempt to separate business operations from host countries' civic and humanitarian responsibilities. Cross-cultural experts believe that ethics is a system of beliefs that supports morality. Moral value systems involve cognitive standards of understanding by which people are judged right or wrong–especially in relationships with other people. Ethical value systems are also known as functions for making decisions that balance competitive demands.

Organizational behavior researchers have embraced the concept of cultural value systems to study such focal topics as a major commitment (Pascal, 1985: 26-41), socialization (Schein, 1968: 1-15), and turnover (O'Reilly, Caldwell, and Barnett, 1989: 21-37). When a company changes its exporting functions to a global market, in most occasions it establishes manufacturing, distribution channels, marketing, and sales facilities abroad. In such a transitional stage, analyzing the cultural and ethical value systems leads us to question certain commonly held beliefs about a company's culture. As Harrison and Carroll (1991: 552) indicate: "For instance, very rapid organizational growth sometimes facilitates rather than impedes cultural stability, when stability is viewed as the quickness with which the system reaches equilibrium or rebounds to it after perturbation."

When a company becomes multinational, it creates *miniatures* of itself in the host countries. These companies are staffed by other nationals and gain a wide degree of autonomy. In practice, it will often be quite difficult to classify the predominant value systems in a globalized corporation. However, it should be relatively easy to identify the sources of the value systems at home and in the host countries.

In globalization of a multinational corporation, there is a fundamental requirement for definition and classification of most conceptual and practical value systems which reflect the central elements defining the general producer and consumer rights. Since these values are central to the concepts of cultural, ethical and legal practices of businesses, the definitions and classification of value systems should be internationally known through the international business practices. Furthermore, focusing on a unified well-defined international value system within the community of nations permits the examination of the likely effects of different types of sub-value systems on both national and corporate value cultures. Focusing on the following three value-based dimensions of cultural, ethical and legal practices are particularly useful for legitimization of international business operations.

TODAY'S INTERNATIONAL BUSINESS ENVIRONMENTS

International businesses do not exist in a vacuum. They arise out of the necessity of home and host countries. The host countries are in need for particular products or services and the home country is in need of market expansion, product diversification, increasing in sales and profits, seeking low cost operation, and exploiting growth opportunities. As a result, international businesses must constantly be aware of the key variables in their environments. There are some factors which are very important to understand the nature of all kind of international business entities. These factors are ownership, investment, management and controlling systems, marketing segmentation, subsidiaries' autonomy, and consumers' lifestyles. For the clarity of the terms used in this text, briefly, you will find definitions of international business entities.

Global Corporations

A *Global Corporation* is a business entity which obtains the factors of production from all countries without restriction and/or discrimination against by both home and host countries and markets its products and/or services around the globe for the purpose of profits (e.g., The World Bank Group and The International Finance Corporation–IFC). These organizations around the globe serve their investors, managers, employees and consumers regardless of their socio-political and economic differences.

Multinational Corporations

A *Multinational Corporation* (MNC) is a highly developed organization with deep worldwide involvement in obtaining the factors of production from multiple countries around the world, and manufactures its products and markets them in specific international markets (e.g., Exxon in Energy; General Motors in Automobiles; Mitsui & Co., Ltd. in Wholesaler; IBM in Computers; E. I. du Pont de Neours in Chemicals; and General Electric in Electrical Equipment).

International Corporations

An *International Corporation* (IC) is a domestic entity which operates its production activities in full-scale at home and markets its products and/or services beyond its national geographic and/or political borders. In return it imports the value added monetary incomes to its country. It engages in exporting goods, services, and management.

Foreign Corporations

A *Foreign Corporation* (FC) is a business entity which has its assets invested by a group of foreigners to operate its production system and markets its products and/or services in host countries for the purpose of making profits. These corporations are controlled and managed by foreigners to the extent in which to adhere to all rules and regulations of the host countries (e.g., Japanese Sanva Bank in the United States).

Transnational Corporations

A *Transnational Corporation* (TNC) refers to an organization whose *management* and *ownership* are divided equally among two or more nations. These corporations acquire their factors of production around the world and market them in specific countries (e.g., Royal Dutch/Shell Group which its headquarters are located in the Netherlands and the United Kingdom). This term is most commonly used by the European countries.

CORPORATE PARADIGM MANAGEMENT SCALE

Parhizgar (1995: 145) constructed a matrix model as a foundational philosophy for analyzing the application of the corporate paradigm management scale (CPMS) (see Figure 1). The two dimensional value-based matrix system helps simplify the analysis of the complex CPMS. Not surprisingly, several of these scales have been applied for analysis of corporate cultural, ethical and legal value systems. In an international endeavor, the problem is the components of the CPMS matrix have not typically been based on global views. These components do not match with the shared values that form the core concepts of international business. Rather, they have been formulated with a broad range of variables based upon corporate national-origin cultural philosophy.

THE FOCUS
ON UNIVERSAL ETHICAL VALUE SYSTEMS

In a global business process, ethics can be a misleading perception because different nations perceive ethical value systems differently. Ethical perception is an individual's belief about what is right and wrong, good and bad, just and unjust, and fair and unfair. Note that ethical and moral beliefs in a culture are rules or standards governing the quality behavior of individual members of a profession, group, or society–not a specific organization. American businesses, in the 1970s and 1980s, were full of such accounts. The big scandals such as the Lockheed Company's bribery, Michael Milken and Ivan Boesky became examples of unethical and in most cases illegal practices of doing business in the United States and abroad (Stewart, 1991: B1; and Arenson, 1986: 8F).

For example, on September 30, 1982, three people in the Chicago area died from cyanide introduced into their Tylenol Extra-Strength

FIGURE 1. Corporate Paradigm Management Scale (CPMS)

	Cultural	Ethical	Legal
Corporate Behavior and Human Relations	How do we relate ourselves with others for mutual understanding?	How are we committed to the human rights globally?	How do we conduct legitimized business?
Corporate Culture and Leadership	How do we promote leadership growth successfully?	How do we perceive doing right things rightly?	How do we strive for effective cross-legal adjustments?
Corporate Strategy and Structure	How do we thrive in times of unpredictable change?	How do we allocate and align right resources?	How do we respect discipline within the work-place?
Corporate Technology and Innovations	How do we strive for problem solving through technological innovation?	How do we inspire the promotion of constructive technologies?	How do we promote cooperative and joint venturing efforts in R & D?
Corporate Politics and Diplomacy	How do we integrate various socio-cultural differences?	How do we proliferate global market models with ethical integrity?	How do we legitimize corporate policies with the global legal environment?
Corporate Economics and Finance	How do we utilize sources and resources productively?	How do we adopt right systems and processes to global competitive conditions?	How do we maintain and respect global copy rights, patents, and property rights?

Source: Parhizgar, K.D. (1995). "Creating Cultural Paradigm Structures for Globalized Corporate Management Ethics." In Evans, J.R., Berman, B., and Barak, B. (Eds.). <u>Proceedings: 1995 Research Conference on Ethics and Social Responsibility in Marketing.</u> Homestead, New York: Frank G. Zarb School of Business, Hofstra University Press, p. 145.

capsules. Johnson & Johnson Pharmaceutical Company, the manufacturer of Tylenol, a leading pain-reliever, did not know whether the cyanide had been introduced into the Tylenol bottles during the manufacturing process or later. The U.S. Food and Drug Administration (FDA), immediately had issued a warning to the public not to take Tylenol. These human deaths reported in the U.S., and possibly outside the United States, caused Johnson & Johnson Corporation to recall and remove all Tylenol bottles from the market. Its cost was more than $100 million. The loss was not covered by *insurance.* The company put the safety of the public first, as the company's credo says it should. The mission of the Johnson & Johnson credo, as reported earlier in this chapter, states: "We believe our first responsibility is to the doctors, nurses, and patients, to mothers, and all others who use our products and services" (*Chicago Tribune, New York Times,* and *Business Week,* 1982).

By using unscrupulous means an executive manager can concede the highest value and accepts the necessity of corporate responsibility to give weight to the ethical issues by the virtue of indicating that the means of the public safety are more important than ends of a corporation.

The major implication in global business is that people with different beliefs will have different ethical standards. Therefore, ethical considerations are relative, not absolute standards of human thoughts and behaviors for all people. Ethical behavior and conduct in global business transactions depend upon the belief systems of producers and consumers. Whether or not a behavior of a person is ethical depends on whom this focus is viewing and who is judging. There is no single best way to ensure that a corporate manager can make ethical decisions. Written codes of conduct often look great, but they may have no effect if employees do not believe or feel that top management takes the codes of ethics seriously.

Ethical considerations are just some of the multitude of factors that influence decision making in organizations. A company lives or dies on its ethical decisions and actions over a long period of time. The difficulty of understanding global business ethics is what worries people the most, due to the fact that they do not know what they are getting into. Are they making the right decisions? Will they get into further troubles? By understanding corporate ethical value systems, the worries will be relieved because employees will know that they will be making the right decisions boldly and confidently.

In the past, many portfolio investors chose to be passive instead of active stockholders. Investors are beginning to pressure corporations with tactics such as media exposure and government attention. Some have formed a class of corporate owners called *shareholder activists.* These people pressure corporate managers to boost profits and dividends. For example, in the 1990s a number of CEOs from major multinational corporations–IBM, General Motors, Apple, and Eastman Kodak, to name a few–have been expelled by dissatisfied stockholders (Fabrikant, 1995, p. 9). Now that the markets are swollen, and many people have their life savings, retirement funds, and other monies, people have awakened up and realized that they must take an active role in their investments.

Nowadays, international stock-market investors are very sensitive to the behaviors of global corporate chief executive officers (CEOs). Officers lose patience when they observe that their employment is on the line. Therefore, they react with swift action to sell their stockholdings for a minimal profit margin rather than letting the stocks mature and then sell them for a substantial amount of profit.

THE FOCUS
ON NATIONAL LEGAL VALUE SYSTEMS

The rule for doing business in a global market has changed drastically. Those corporations who understand the new international rules for doing business in a free world economy will prosper; those who cannot may perish (Mohrman and Mitroff, 1987: 37). Like people, rules and regulations have an origin. But the international regulatory process is not widely understood and practiced by nations. Usually in industrialized societies, the government's regulatory life cycle first begins with the emergence of an acute issue. Second is the formulation of government policy. Third is the implementation of the legislation. Then, these rules and regulations will be circulated internationally.

Business operations and trade transactions are monitored and, when necessary, informal or formal corrective actions are taken. It is not easy to portray the magnitude of global business and the sheer volume of regulations to which global businesses are subject. The international business rules and regulations are very complex. For example, on December 3, 1984, the Union Carbide Pesticide plant in Bhopal, India faced a problem when a sequence of procedures and devices failed. Fugitive lethal vapors crossed the plant boundaries, killing 4,037 people and seriously caused injury to 60,000 people around the plant. The lethal gas leak had been called one of the worst industrial-mass disasters ever after the release of radionuclides by a Russian reactor at Chernobyl in the Ukraine in 1985. The Ukrainian authorities estimated that radiation deaths totaled 125,000 and elevated death rates will continue in the next decades because of latency periods for radiation-induced illnesses (Williams, 1995: A4). The catastrophes at Chernobyl, Ukraine and Bhopal, India were on international manifestation of some fundamentally wrong actions by governments and businesses in the modern time (Weir, 1987: xii). Who should and could be blamed for such catastrophes? Were the former Soviet Union and Indian governments at fault? Was the Bhopal incident the Union Carbide Company's fault? And/or was it the United Nations' World Health Organization–WHO and/or the United Nations Atomic Energy Commissioner's deficiency?

THE FOCUS
ON CORPORATE MULTICULTURAL VALUE SYSTEMS

The primary focus of a global corporation is based upon cultural values concerning functions performed for, and relations with international organizations, governments' representatives as well as consumers. In a cultural value system, either universal or regional, the major concern is focusing on contexts of issues (Swierczek, 1988: 76). Managerial and organizational cultures are concerned with the particular environmental conditions or sets of problems in which skills, techniques, and approaches are applied. The key questions about managerial and organizational cultures could be raised as: "Are these applications appropriately designed with circumstances or fixed-value systems?" and "Is the managerial and organizational framework of cultural value systems on which these applications are based consistent with the framework of value systems in the situation in which the applications are made?" These and other questions raise several issues about legitimacy of a national cultural value system within the context of the international environment. If management culture is universal, then the transfer of techniques will be culturally compatible. If management culture is a national phenomenon, one must make greater efforts to transform these approaches during the globalization process regardless of their cultural heritage or origin of these cultural value systems. For example, consider that a manufacturer who wishes to survive in a very intensive competitive market feels that in order to do so he/she must bribe a potential foreign government authority in order to sell his/her products. Is there any similar cultural and/or ethical rule according to both home and host countries? In these situations we must consider the international rule, "to bribe," and/or "to be bribed," is not a universal practice. If we attempt to universalize the rule involved, we quickly perceive that it is self-contradictory. In the event, if the bribery has not been made a universal rule, then bribery would not be a universal way of doing business. The main argument is in the case when managerial culture is universal, then organizational cultures could be different. In order for a universal management culture to be effective, there should be similarities in the organizational cultural value systems with the universal managerial value systems. Then the end-result in a managerial culture becomes universal.

Global strategy and structure are important, but the heart of a global organization is its corporate culture. It is the means through which global strategies and structures are executed in order to ensure global competitiveness and profitability. A global corporate culture comprises the mission, vision, values, beliefs, expectations, and both conceptual and perceptual attitudes of its members. Most domestic firms find that their greatest weakness is their difficulty to change their corporate cultural value systems to compete in globalized markets. It is becoming clear to researchers, that Japanese and European corporate cultures and management practices put much greater efforts over a much longer period of time into developing global corporate cultures and human resources than do U.S. companies (Rhinesmith, 1991: 131- 137). For example, the corporate cultural value systems of the Japanese are very different from those of the U.S. Eccles (1991: 131-137) indicates that during the 1980s many executives saw their companies' success decline, because global competitors seized their market shares.

In order to succeed as a profit-making organization, multinational corporations must move towards a task-alignment form which is reengineering the organizational task force and employees' roles, reinventing corporate responsibilities, and reenergizing corporate relations with customers to solve specific global business problems (Beer et al., 1990: 158-166). Therefore, to be an effective global corporation, top management must strive for changing the cultural, ethical, and legal attitudes of all stakeholders within their organizational context. Employees must be informed of the problems affecting and dragging the organization into a profitless market environment. Since an organization consists of hundreds of individuals and different departments, both employees and employers are required to enforce organizational cultural, ethical, and legal value systems. In sum, the corporate management discipline system should eliminate improper occurrences of unethical and illegal conducts and promptly provide suitable alternatives in order to match with their legitimized corporate mission. However, employees must recognize that in almost all cases of difficulties, they are part of the problem and a great deal of the solution. Employers and employees in a competitive global marketplace and market-space must understand who they really are. Therefore, multinational corporations should strive for discovery of their strengths and weaknesses and then try to convert weaknesses to strengths.

CONCLUSION

This article has spelled out exactly what is meant by *multicultural behavior* and *multinational management,* and outlined the general perspectives and objectives of this new field. Then it turned to brief historical transitions of business transactions and organizational decision-making processes. The ethical, moral, and legal implications of multicultural value systems have been analyzed. All of these observations have vast and profound implications for multinational management and the future of business enterprises. Currently, the management of multinational corporations is significantly different from what the domestic corporate management was a few years ago.

Everyone should be concerned about multicultural human behavior. The field of multicultural behaviorism has the goals of understanding, prediction, and assimilating an individual's conceptions into a pluralistic one. The multicultural management is providing appropriate room for all organizational members to appreciate their value systems in congruence with other organizational members toward synergy.

REFERENCES

Arenson, K.W. (1986). "How Wall Street Bred Ivan Boesky." *New York Times* November 26), p. 8F.

Bass, B.M., Burger, P.C., Doktor, R., and Barrett, G.V. (1979). *Assessment of Managers: An International Comparison.* New York: The Free Press.

Beer, M. et al. (1990). "Why Change Programs Don't Produce Change." *Harvard Business Review,* Vol. 68, No. 6, pp. 158-166.

Business Week, October 18, 1982.

Chen, C. and Eastman, W. (1997). "Toward a Civic Culture for Multicultural Organizations." *Journal of Applied Behavioral Science.* Vol.33, No. 4, pp. 454-470.

Chicago Tribune, December 1997, October 1-10, 1982.

Copeland, L. (1988). "Valuing Diversity, Part 1: Making the Most of Cultural Differences at Workplace." *Personnel* (June), Vol. 65, No. 6, p. 52.

Cox, Jr., T. (1993). *Cultural Diversity in Organizations: Theory, Research and Practice.* San Francisco: Berrett-Koehler Publishers, pp. 1 & 6.

De George, R.T. (1995). *Business Ethics.* Fourth Edition. Englewood Cliffs, New Jersey: Prentice Hall, p. 14.

de Vries, S. (1992). *Working in Multi-Ethnic Groups: The Performance and Well Being of Minority and Majority Workers.* Amsterdam: Gouda Quint bu–Arnhem.

Drucker, P. (1980). *Managing in Turbulent Times.* New York: Harper and Row, Publishers, pp. 190-194.

Eccles, R.G. (1991). "The Performance Measurement Manifesto." *Harvard Business Review,* Vol. 69, No. 1, pp. 131-137.

Eiteman, D.K., and Stonehill, A.I. (1979). *Multinational Business Finance.* 2nd Ed. Reading, MA: Addison-Wesley, pp. 1-2.

Fabrikat, G. (1995). "Battling for Hearts and Minds at Time Warner." *New York Times,* February 26, p. 9.

Fernandez, J.P. (1991). *Managing a Diverse Work Force: Regaining the Competitive Edge.* Lexington, MA: Lexington Books, p. 71.

Friedman, M. (1971). "Does Business Have a Social Responsibility?" *Bank Administration* (April).

Fullerton, H.N. (1987). "Labor Force Projections: 1986-2000." *Monthly Labor Review,* pp. 19-29.

Gudykunst, W.B. (1994). *Bridging Differences: Effective Intergroup Communication.* Thousand Oaks, CA: Sage.

Gordon, M.W. (1993). *Doing Business in Mexico.* New York: Transnational Juris Publications, Inc., Part II, Chapter 3, p. 6.

Harrison, J.R. and Caroll, G.R. (1991). "Keeping the Faith: A Model of Cultural Transmission in Formal Organizations." *Administrative Science Quarterly,* pp. 552-582.

Harvey, C. and M.J. Allard (1995). *Understanding Diversity: Readings, Cases, and Exercises.* New York: Harper Collins College Publishers, p. 3.

Hill, J., and Dulek, R. (1993). "A Miss Manners Guide to Doing Business in Europe." *Business Horizon,* Vol. 36, No. 4 (July/August Edition), pp. 551-52.

Hofstede, G. (1980a). *Culture's Consequences: International Differences in Work Related Values.* Beverly Hills: Sage Publications.

Hofstede, G. (1980b). "Motivation, Leadership, and Organizations: Do American Theories Apply Abroad?" *Organizational Dynamics* (Summer), pp. 42-63.

Hofstede, G. (1993). "Cultural Constrains in Management Theories." *Academy of Management Executive*, Vol. 7 No. 1, (February Edition), pp. 81-94.

Horwitz, T., and Forman, C. (1990). "Clashing Cultures." *The Wall Street Journal*, p. A1.

International Financial Statistics (IMF), (1998).

Jackson, J.H., Miller, R.L., and Miller, S.G. (1997). *Business and Society Today: Managing Social Issues.* New York: West Publishing Company, p. 172.

Jackson Grayson, C. and O'Dell, C. (1988). *American Business: A Two Minute Warning.* New York: The Free Press, pp. 8-9.

Johnson, R.B., and O'Mara, J. (1992). "Shedding Light on Diversity Training." *Training and Diversity* (May), pp. 45-52.

Johnston, W. (1991). "Global Work Force 2000: The New World Labor Market." *Harvard Business Review* (March/April), Vol. 69, 115-127.

Kirrane, D.F. (1990). "Managing Values: A Systematic Approach to Business Ethics." *Training and Development Journal* (November), pp. 53-60.

Kolberg, W.H. and Smith, F.C.(1992). *Rebuilding America's Work-Force: Business Strategies to Close the Competitive Gap.* Homewood, IL: Irwin, p. 17.

Laurent, A. (1983). "The Cultural Diversity of Western Corporations of Management." *International Studies of Management and Organization*, Vol. XIII, No. 1-2 (Spring-Summer), pp. 75-96.

Marquardt, M.J., and Engel, D.W. (1993). "HRD Competencies for a Shrinking World." *Training and Development* (May), Vol. 47, No. 5, p. 59.

Martin, J. (1993). *Culture in Organizations.* New York: Oxford University Press.

Mohrman, S.A. and Mitroff, I.I. (1987). "Business Not As Usual." *Training and Development Journal*, Vol. 41, No. 6, pp. 37-34.

Moran, R.T., and Harris, P.R. *Managing Cultural Synergy.* Houston: Gulf Publishing Company, pp. 5, 157.

New York Times, October 1-10, 1982.

O'Reilly, C.A., III, Caldwell, D.F., and Barnett, W.P. (1989). "Work Group Demography, Social Integration and Turnover." *Administrative Science Quarterly*, Vol. 34, pp. 21-37.

Parhizgar, K.D., and Jesswein, K.R. (1995). "Socio-Ethical And Economic Fairness-Affordability of Developing Nations' Repayment of International Debt." In Fatemi, K. and Nichols, S.E.W. (1995). *International Business in the 21st Century.* Vol. II, pp. 463-473.

Parhizgar, K.D. (1995). "Creating Cultural Paradigm Structure for Globalized Corporate Management Ethics." In Evans, J.R., Berman, B., and Benny Barak (Eds.). *Proceedings: 1995 Research Conference on Ethics and Social Responsibility in Marketing.* New York: Hofstra University Press, pp. 137-150.

Pascal, R.T., (1985). "The Paradox of Corporate Culture." *California Management Review*, Vol. 27, No. 2, pp. 26-41.

Rhinesmith, S.H. (1991). "An Agenda for Globalization." *Training and Development Journal* (February), Vol. 45, No. 2, pp. 24-27 and 131-137.

Riche, M.F. (1991). "We're All Minorities Now." *American Demographics* (October), Vol. 13, No. 10, p. 34.

Schein, E.H. (1968). "Organizational Socialization and the Profession of Management." *Industrial Management Review*, Vol. 9, pp. 1-15.

Solomon, C.M. (1993). "Managing Today's Immigrants." *Personnel Journal.* February, 1993, p. 58.

Stewart, J.B. (1991). "Scenes From a Scandal: The Secret World of Michael and Ivan Boeskey." *Wall Street Journal.* (October 2), p. B1.

Swierczek, F. (1988). "Cultural and training: How Do They Play Away From Home?" *Training and Development Journal*, Vol. 42, No. 11, p. 76.

Weir, D. (1987). *The Bhopal Syndrome.* San Francisco: Sierra Club Books, p. xii.

Williams, C.J. (1995). "9 Years Later, Chernobyl Disaster Look Worse." *Los Angeles Times* (April 27), p. A4.

World Investment Report: An Executive Summary (1993). United Nations Conference on Trade and Development Program On Transnational Corporations. New York: United Nations Publications, pp. 1-4.

Yankelovich, D. (1982). "The Work Ethic is Underemployed." *Psychology Today,* May, pp. 5-8.

Social Resources:
The Role of Patriates
in the Expatriate Experience

Madeline Crocitto
Maali Ashamalla

SUMMARY. This paper advances the ideas that host country nationals, i.e., patriates, constitute an important part of the social environment of an expatriate. Social network theory is used to provide a framework from which to examine expatriate-patriate relationships on the individual, dyad, and group levels. Specifically, it is proposed that expatriate-patriate links, as well as characteristics of the social group in which the expatriate exists, contribute to expatriate effectiveness through their help with shaping work and nonwork networks of information and contacts. It is also recommended that where appropriate, patriate expertise be incorporated into human resource decisions related to the expatriation process. Suggestions on how to accomplish this integration are also offered. *[Article copies available for a fee from The Haworth Document Delivery Service: 1-800-342-9678. E-mail address: getinfo@haworthpressinc. com <Website: http://www.haworthpressinc.com>]*

The opportunities of globalization are accompanied by challenges, not the least of which is the effective adaptation and performance of

Madeline Crocitto is affiliated with the State University of New York at Old Westbury, 400 Atlantic Avenue East Rockaway, NY 11518 (E-mail: MMCrocitto@ aol.com).

Maali Ashamalla is affiliated with Indiana College of Pennsylvania, Eberly College of Business, Indiana, PA 15701 (E-mail: Ashamala@grove.iup.edu).

The authors appreciate the comments of Shawn Carraher, Necla Geyikdagi, Yasar Geyikdagi, and Malcolm Hayward on an earlier version of this paper.

[Haworth co-indexing entry note]: "Social Resources: The Role of Patriates in the Expatriate Experience." Crocitto, Madeline, and Maali Ashamalla. Co-published simultaneously in *Journal of Transnational Management Development* (International Business Press, an imprint of The Haworth Press, Inc.) Vol. 4, No. 3/4, 1999, pp. 25-44; and: *Culture and International Business* (ed: Kip Becker) International Business Press, an imprint of The Haworth Press, Inc., 2000, pp. 25-44. Single or multiple copies of this article are available for a fee from The Haworth Document Delivery Service [1-800-342-9678, 9:00 a.m. - 5:00 p.m. (EST). E-mail address: getinfo@haworthpressinc.com].

25

the expatriate in a foreign assignment. The failure of the expatriate manager to adjust to the foreign environment is a major problem for many U.S. organizations. Anywhere from 25% to 40% of all expatriates from the U.S. have failed (Ralston, Terpstra, Cunniff & Gustafson, 1995). These failure rates are much higher than those from Europe and Asia ("Don't Be An Ugly American," 1995; Tung, 1987). The implications of this are even more important today, with foreign assignments accompanying increasing global strategic alliances (Mervosh & McClenahen, 1997), especially when no local talent is available ("Benchmarking for Placement," 1998). With the realization of the career set-backs incurred by the expatriate and the crucial role expatriates play in the success of international expansion, closer attention needs to be given to the expatriate experience.

Expatriate success and failure can be attributed to performance based on ability and adjustment measured as the "fit" of an individual to the new cultural environment. Failure of international assignments may take the form of lower performance or early return to the home country (Takeuchi, 1997). In addition, the expatriate may eschew the mandates and needs of headquarters in favor of those of the host country facility, or may leave a particular location, job, or the organization (Birdseye & Hill, 1995). The actual costs of unsatisfactory expatriate assignments are substantial, with the average cost of expatriates usually from three to four times the salary of the individual (Gates, 1996). An increasing number of companies enter into contracts with employees in which the employer is reimbursed for relocation and other costs should the expatriate prematurely leave the assignment ("Are You Entitled," 1998).

Besides this potential financial expense, the individual expatriate also incurs substantial careers costs in terms of diminished reputation, lower self-confidence, less challenging assignments, and turnover. The costs to the individual may be especially acute in the environment of the boundaryless career, where one is judged by success on the latest projects, and in which networking and one's reputation are crucial (Arthur & Rousseau, 1996).

This paper addresses the expatriation process by changing our perspective of an unsuccessful expatriate assignments as either an individual employee and/or a human resource management deficiency. We start with the premise that the expatriation process should be viewed beyond the limited perspective of the individual expatriate to that of the social context in which the expatriate works and lives. There is a need for a comprehensive model of expatriation which would include societal cultural dimensions, organizational factors such as the size, purpose, and prior performance of the facility, and the individual expatriate demographic and psychological factors. We believe that taking a holistic view of the expatriate experience by further examining the socialization process of the expatriate and his/her family to their new environment, will offer valuable insight into the dynamics of international assignments. This paper makes the following contributions:

- Provides a rationale for going beyond the individual level of analysis to examining the social context of expatriation as reasons for success or failure.
- Offers a conceptual framework applicable to both the adjustment and performance aspects of the expatriate assignment.
- Suggests ways to enhance the expatriate experience by including the input of employees of the host country national facility, which we call patriates, in human resource decisions.

In the first part of this paper, we use concepts from social network theory to develop a more comprehensive perspective of the expatriation process than currently exists. Our approach includes considering host country nations (i.e., patriates), expatriates, as well as the social system in which they both operate. The second part of this paper is concerned with how patriates can contribute to various types of human resource decisions about expatriate staffing and adjustment.

NETWORKS

A network is a specific set of persons, objects, or events that are linked through types of relationships. In a network of individuals, relationships include those based on communication, boundary penetration, instrumentality, sentiment, power, and authority. Network theory is based on the premise that the structure of these relationships and the location of an individual in a network has significant behavioral, perceptual, and attitudinal consequences for individuals who make up the network (Knoke & Kuklinski, 1982). In an organization, formal networks are those assigned for the purpose of accomplishment. Informal networks also emerge and may or may not be related to formal networks. These informal structures are helpful for task accomplishments; their properties may explain the difference between high and low performing individuals and groups (Ibarra, 1992).

Expatriate Networks

A meaningful understanding of the expatriate's experience can be gained by studying the networks of the expatriate's social system within the host country's facility. We propose that parent company personnel and host country nationals should be proactive in assisting the expatriate to develop networks. People choose to associate with similar others (Burt, 1992). An expatriate from another country and facility newly introduced to a host country national work group is noticeably dissimilar from the other group members. If the expatriate is from headquarters and is sent as the top manager of the host country facility, there is ample dissimilarity in work experience, organizational level and personal background to make network building difficult. It is important that the parent company and host country facility participate in developing networks for the expatriate to use as resources in handling work and nonwork issues. Network building involves selecting individuals to be in the network and understanding how they are contacted. Having a wide range of people to connect with provides resources related to one's effectiveness in terms of access to information, knowledge of information flows, and a time advantage (Burt, 1992).

The goals of the parent company and host country facility are potentially advanced when the expatriate builds the personal contacts necessary for network formation. One way to initiate this process is for the host country facility to provide the expatriate with introductions to several employees of the facility. These individuals would be available to help the expatriate in connecting to numerous work groups and also provide various kinds of information.

Levels of Analysis

Prior research in the area of expatriation has taken place at two levels. One is that of the solo expatriate sent to a facility in a foreign country. The other is more recent and focuses on the international work team. Areas that warrant closer attention are the socialization processes of the expatriate in the foreign operation and the properties of the group the expatriate must work with in order to fulfill job responsibilities. The traditions of understanding human behavior and performance by examining the individual-group relationships and group processes are useful in understanding the expatriate experience.

Network theory suggests examining the roles and characteristics of individuals and groups along three levels of analysis. This paper offers an analysis of expatriation at these levels: (1) the individual level, in which the position of an individual within a network is judged in relation to the characteristics of the individual and other group members, including the frequency and type of relationships between that individual and network members; (2) the dyad level, in which pairs of individuals are examined for common or variant characteristics, and the frequency and nature of their relationship; and (3) the group level, in which the entire network group is analyzed through linkages among all group members pertaining to frequency of interaction, the nature of the interaction, and common characteristics (Burt, 1992). The following sections discuss the expatriate experience at each of these levels.

The Individual Level of Analysis
(The Individual–Group Connection)

The literature at the individual level reveals that successful expatriates possess various qualities. These include (1) balanced loyalties to the parent company and the host national facility (Black & Gregersen, 1992); (2) cultural awareness, adaptability, flexibility, tolerance of ambiguity, physical stamina, a sense of humor, stress management, and interpersonal and intercultural competence (Odenwald, 1996); (3) proficiency in the language of the host country (Dolainski, 1997); and (4) some international travel experience (Antal, 1993). In our view, we need to go beyond characteristics of the individual because socialization cannot occur outside the context of interpersonal and group experiences.

We start our examination at the individual level by viewing the expatriate as a newcomer to the social environment of the existing network (i.e., work group). Although networks may not be confined to groups, we use the words networks and groups interchangeably in order to draft our points in general terms.

Network theory suggests we consider individuals as roleholders possessing various characteristics. The network concepts we believe to be appropriate in analyzing the expatriate experience are whether the individual is prominent in a network and whether the individual occupies a gatekeeper role. These are especially salient for the manager who is sent overseas to run the operation. We assume the expatriate possesses a high level of responsibility and authority in the new assignment, and so our discussion centers on the expatriate as the focal point of the network.

An individual manager controls information and resources by occupying a leadership position. Others in the workgroup are required to direct their relationships towards him or her in order to accomplish their job tasks. Therefore, a manager, by virtue of his/her position, is *prominent* as a person who is extensively the object of relationships with other network members (Knoke & Burt, 1983). Prominence creates visibility to those inside and outside the group, magnifying the manager's success and failure. It may be difficult for a newcomer to easily become prominent in a culturally different work group. An expatriate manager who is ignored or otherwise rejected by group members does not attain prominence.

Providing the expatriate with a group of willing potential network members as "coaches" available for various types of work and nonwork advice and information creates more immediate linkages than an individual could develop on his/her own. The greater the number of linkages, the greater the density of a network. Density in terms of actual to total possible connections improves the reachability of the expatriate to newcomers and vice versa. Pre-established connections reduce the number of steps the expatriate moves through to obtain information (Scott, 1991). Both the expatriate and the patriates benefit by the ability to reach each other without relying on the grapevine and hearsay. Little connection to flows of information may lengthen the adjustment period, exacerbate communication problems, and lead to performance difficulties. Figure 1 represents a basic depiction of an undirected network, where the direction of information flows is reciprocal between the expatriate and each patriate.

Much of the literature refers to expatriate adjustment at work; less attention is given to nonwork adaptation which impacts on performance and satisfaction with the assignment (Sievers, 1998). A dense network of contacts should increase the rate of adjustment for the entire expatriate family. Possible information about the work and nonwork environment which may be gained by the expatriate manager

FIGURE 1. The Prominent Expatriate Managers (Undirected Network)

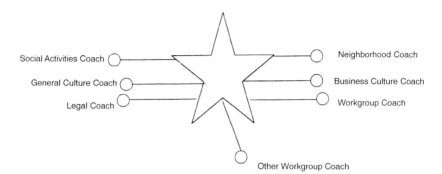

through networking also appears in Figure 1. In sociometric terms, the expatriate is depicted as a star, or someone who is a focal point (Scott, 1991). Each circle represents a group member acting as a coach with a responsibility for information in a particular area. Some of these areas relate to task attainment in terms of business culture; others relate to such general life concerns as cultural norms, neighborhood characteristics, educational information, and social activities. We assume that access to necessary information will result in better adjustment which will help enhance the stature of the expatriate manager.

The second network role relevant to the study of the individual expatriate is that of a *gatekeeper* who links the network to external domains (Tichy, Tushman & Fombrun, 1979). As the center or star of the network, the expatriate can link to other disconnected groups such as personnel at headquarters, resource providers, other facilities, and local markets and organizations. This allows for resource flows and strengthens the company's culture. The expatriate, by definition, links the host country facility to various entities. Providing such connections without prior host country experience can be difficult. It is more time consuming for the expatriate to learn about the internal workings of the new facility and external associations without the assistance of experienced patriates. The expatriate as a gatekeeper, represented by a star in the diagram, connects the patriates with the parent company and builds contacts with groups such as other branches, suppliers, and customers (see Figure 2).

Prominence and gatekeeping can be facilitated if patriates with expertise in distinctive areas and knowledge of external groups are assigned to the expatriate, especially at the beginning of the assignment. Having a set of available individuals for help shortens the learning curve to be mastered by the expatriate.

The Dyad Level
(Individual Expatriate-Individual Patriate Connection)

Pair-wise or dyadic linkages have not been investigated in studies of expatriate adjustment. Although mentoring involves a dyadic relationship, it usually occurs with both parties in the same location. However, mentoring of expatriates differs in that the mentor is usually at the home office and the expatriate protege is at an overseas location. Typically, the mentor has not experienced first-hand the expatriate's role in a particular facility and location. On-site relationships should be considered as important to successful expatriation. Evidence from a study of 179 expatriates of one company in 22 countries demonstrated that on-site mentoring in professional and psycho-social areas helped expatriate socialization. This was positively manifested in job satisfac-

FIGURE 2. The Expatriate as Gatekeeper–Highest Ranking Roleholder

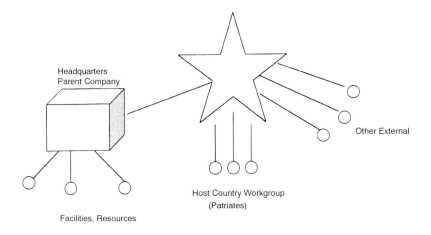

tion, plans to complete the assignment, and better comprehension of international business (Feldman & Bolin, 1997).

Mentoring of an expatriate may be difficult to develop at the host country location. There may be no one to serve as an on-site mentor, especially when the expatriate is sent as the manager of the facility with no organizational levels above him/her. Also, mentoring is a somewhat intense relationship that develops on a mutual basis over a period of time. The relatively shorter amount of time an expatriate spends at a facility along with performance pressures may preclude the longitudinal development of an on-going mentoring relationship. Katz and Seifer (1996) recommend that a support network of repatriated employees, senior expatriates, and new expatriates be established so that various types of information and psychosocial support are available.

As proposed earlier, we submit that rather than a single mentor, several informal patriate coaches be appointed to the expatriate, especially before the actual assignment begins. The number of coaches and the nature of their dyadic relationship to the expatriate would be determined by the expatriate's needs and the coaches' abilities and knowledge. These coaches serve as reference points for questions and concerns from the expatriate before departure to the international assignment and continue to serve as coaches after the expatriate arrives. In network terms, these patriate coaches serve as bridges. A *bridge* roleholder can broker, access, and control information (Knoke & Burt, 1983). We suggest the organization designate these individuals as helpful suppliers of various types of information. Through them, the expatriate would have access to a wider range of information, experience, attitudes, and suggestions from which to make decisions. A greater range of information and advice provided by bridges should improve the quality of the expatriate's decisions, enhance performance, and promote adjustment to the new environment. Coaching may moderate the expatriate's culture shock, confusion, and potential mistakes. It may eventually develop into a mentoring relationship. This is especially important at the beginning of an assignment.

Another advantage to the appointment of several coaches to the expatriate is that it aids in building social capital. Burt (1992) identifies three types of capital: financial capital or resources; human capital or one's knowledge, skill, ability, health, and personal characteristics; and social capital arising from relationships among individuals. The company also gains through the accumulation of social capital across individuals. The organization should carefully select these coaches and recognize their contributions to various forms of capital assets.

Both the expatriate and patriate acquire social capital from participating in a dyadic relation with structural holes. Structural holes exist when contacts are not redundant in that each contact leads to sets of people unconnected to one another (Burt, 1992). Lack of redundancy increases the amount of information and social contacts an individual has access to. It benefits the expatriate to have an array of networks with structural holes via coaches through which to receive and disseminate task and social information. The personal connections of the patriate bridges help those working at the host country facility learn about the expatriate's preferences, plans, background, capabilities, etc. It is more efficient for an individual to devote time and energy to maintain relationships with structural holes, because this would yield the maximum amount of information and contacts.

We propose that the expatriate be assigned to different coach patriates from all levels of the host country facility, each with a distinctive competency, thus providing structural holes. One may be familiar with local laws; another with technological applications; a third with issues relevant to family adjustment in areas such as housing, school systems, shopping, and opportunities for socializing. There is anecdotal support for this approach. In a program offered by Digital Equipment, part of team building training at the company's home office involved assigning each expatriate trainee to a U.S. associate. This included the associate's family who served as bridges to other people and information. This approach was credited with increased efficiency in new product developments (Odenwald, 1996). Shell International has already developed networks of other transferred families in host countries. They are staffed by expatriate spouses who supply extensive information about the new environment (Sievers, 1998).

Strong networks in general and with structural holes in particular, may assist with the nonwork aspects important to expatriate adjustment. One study reported 93% of expatriates valued help in getting accustomed to their new locale (Frazee, 1998). Another issue influencing expatriate adaptation is that of the "trailing spouse" who may be unable to continue his/her career or find employment (Barton & Bishko, 1998). Only a small percentage of spouses receive career assistance; dual-career families who lose the second income may find themselves with a lower standard of living (Fitzgerald-Turner, 1997).

Patriate networks may facilitate employment opportunities and other productive and leisure-time endeavors for a spouse and other family members. Overall then, patriates could greatly ease the adjustment process by helping the entire expatriate family adapt to various aspects of life in a new environment.

The Group Level
(Connections Among Group Members)

Any change in group membership, regardless of the type and purpose of a group, changes the interpersonal dynamics of the social system. In organizations, we expect work groups that are primarily task-oriented and expertise-based to automatically adapt to new members. Cross-cultural issues add to the difficulties of group adjustment. For example, differences between French and Slovenian work groups in terms of language and culture were bridged when a researcher used her knowledge of each culture to dispel misunderstandings between the two groups. This improved the work relationships of the groups and accelerated the modernization of an automobile plant (Globokar, 1996). Without at least one group member familiar with the cultures of other group members, the group may fail to perform productively. Clarke and Lipp (1998) recommend that a bicultural team with extensive knowledge and experience of both cultures, including language fluency, is necessary to prevent misinterpretation and conflict in an international setting. This supports our recommendation that a group of patriates be assigned to assist the expatriate. Although they may not be very familiar with the culture of the expatriate, they can help the expatriate become more aware of their culture. This may be more practical than assembling a bicultural team for just one expatriate. In any case, the individual expatriate does not exist alone, but in the context of the work groups of the host country facility.

One way to determine the potential ease or difficulty of an expatriate's adjustment to an international assignment is to look at the characteristics and relationships of group members. An expatriate who joins a group with an individual or several individuals who can bridge cultures should have a smoother adjustment than someone who struggles alone as an outsider within the group. Analysis of the entire expatriate work group may provide fruitful insights into the process of expatriate adaptation.

Network theory suggests it is possible to draw inferences about group attitudes and behaviors by analyzing the ratio of network members along selected criteria such as characteristics, experiences, or linkages. Using network concepts as a guide, we suggest a better person-group fit for the expatriate might occur if the company examines the inequality, insularity and stability of the work groups that the expatriate is going to be associated with.

Inequality within a group refers to classifying members along a selected criterion to examine the social structure of the group (Tichy, Tushman & Fombrun, 1979). With a new expatriate, it would be helpful to understand the social structure of the groups he/she is joining. Similarity of group member characteristics such as date of entry into the organization has been useful in understanding social structure and socialization. Those groups with similar others are more likely to share views and goals, and to act in coalitions to meet these goals. This similarity increases communication and the attraction of group members to each other (Pfeffer, 1983). Dissimilarity has been associated with increased exits from a group (Wagner, Pfeffer & O'Reilly, 1984). An in-group may relate lack of similarity to perceptions of conflict when considering an out-group (Labianca, Brass & Gray, 1998). Since an expatriate is an outsider he/she may be perceived as a member of an out-group of, perhaps, previous expatriates or visitors from headquarters (see Figure 3).

We propose that the adjustment of the expatriate would be related to the distribution of entry dates of group members into that particular

FIGURE 3. Group Level Network Characteristics

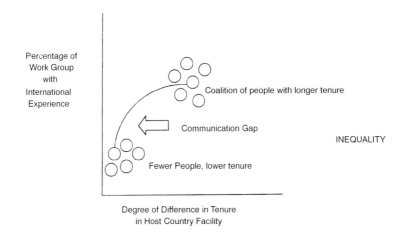

Percentage of
Work Group
with
International
Experience

Coalition of people with longer tenure

Communication Gap

INEQUALITY

Fewer People, lower tenure

Degree of Difference in Tenure
in Host Country Facility

work group, the organization in general, and the amount and type of international experience of group members. An expatriate who enters a group of long-tenured host country nationals with no international background will have a different experience from an expatriate who enters a group with shorter tenures and international exposure. These background variables are measurable and may yield valuable insights into the ease with which an expatriate becomes effective in a particular work setting.

Another network characteristic of a work group is that of *insularity*, which is defined as the ratio of internal to external links of a social unit (Tichy, Tushman & Fombrun, 1979). Insularity denotes a close-knit group with many internal links. It can be reasoned that an expatriate introduced into an insular or closed group composed of people who have only worked at that facility and with little or no international background would find integration into that group problematic (see Figure 4).

Conversely, external links signal openness to environmental changes necessary for adaptation and survival (Aldrich, 1979). In the context of the expatriate experience, we would consider external links from two viewpoints. The first is the proportion of those in the expatriate work group with international work experience. This experience can take many forms beyond working in another country. It may include international education, travel, a multicultural family background, and foreign language or cultural studies. The second is the proportion of group

FIGURE 4. Work Group Distribution–Degree of International Experience

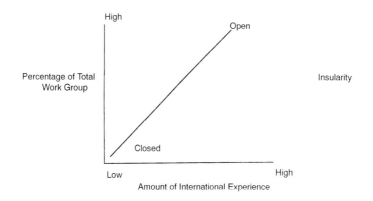

members with work experience outside the company with no international experience. Including individuals with various backgrounds and experiences allows for technology and information transfer, the formulation of new procedures, and diverse methods of information processing. The ideal situation would be if the expatriate joins a group that is open along both dimensions. Group members should more likely be receptive to his/her arrival, tolerant of new ideas and behaviors, and strategically aligned with environmental conditions.

A third network concept, which applies to the expatriate joining an existing work group, is its *stability,* which is the degree to which a network changes the composition of its membership over time (Tichy, Tushman & Fombrun, 1979) (see Figure 5). Variations in personnel are often necessary to bring new information, experiences, and perspectives into an organization. Very stable groups seek to maintain the status quo and may resist change. Therefore, the expatriate who enters a stable work group may find group members resistant to new information and change. As a result, adaptation to the environment is impeded. On the other hand, an unstable group with many new people would lengthen the adjustment time and delay group performance. The optimum situation for fast and full adjustment would be for the expatriate to join a group of average stability. A group with average stability would also have developed some useful patterns of communication and task allocation and be accustomed to integrating new members.

To summarize, the aim of the preceding discussion was to illustrate the potential contribution of the social context of the expatriate's work groups to the success or failure of an overseas assignment. Our major point is that host country nationals or patriates should be included in any examination of the expatriation process. In part one we discussed their involvement with networks. In the following section, we discuss patriates as resource individuals to be consulted when making human resource management decisions related to expatriation when culturally acceptable and practical.

THE ROLE OF PATRIATES
IN INTERNATIONAL HUMAN RESOURCE FUNCTIONS

With approximately 20% of expatriate assignments ending in early exits (Groh & Allen, 1998), poor expatriation decisions can result in substantial human and financial costs. It is our belief that international

FIGURE 5. The Degree of Network Change

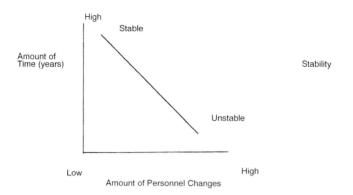

human resource practices can be improved if employees at the host country facility are involved in various decisions concerning expatriation. These individuals are essential to the implementation of a global strategy and are also affected by the company's policies and practices. Participative management is not a new idea nor is it necessarily culturally transferable.

Getting patriates to serve as coaches and mentors may not be easy when the expatriate is assigned as the top manager of the facility, especially in a country that is high on the power distance dimension described by Hofstede (1991). In this situation, social relationships are structured into a hierarchy with emphasis on obeying those with greater authority. However, Katz and Seifer (1995) note in their integration of international dimensions, only the Near Eastern (Greece, Iran, Turkey, and Yugoslavia) and Arab (Saudi Arabia, Kuwait, Oman, Bahrain, Abu-Dhabi, United Arab Emirates) clusters are high on power distance. Even then, they tend to be medium on the individualism-collectivism dimension in terms of obligations to others, and medium on masculinity-femininity which includes regard for others and quality of life issues. This may override the emphasis on social hierarchy, especially outside the confines of work, allowing interested individuals to serve as coaches and mentors. Whether this is the case is yet to be determined empirically. We recommend patriates be involved in international human resources (IHR) functional decisions related to expatriation as explained below.

Planning

If we accept the premise that the person most familiar with a job is the job incumbent, then a patriate employee would provide valuable input about a successor or colleague. The patriate may have had extensive interaction with a potential expatriate and can provide insight into that individual's suitability for assignment to that location. The human resource department should be proactive in building an international human resource information system database to identify and "track" talented individuals for potential overseas assignments. Designated individuals may then be evaluated and receive training and development to eventually qualify for an assignment in another country. Progressive companies such as Eli Lilly & Co. develop a global reservoir of managerial talent ("Lilly Prepares," 1996). Patriates can nominate themselves and/or colleagues to be included in such a database.

Recruiting

Some companies report difficulty in developing a pool of qualified candidates for international assignments (Frazee 1998). One option is to turn to host country nationals who may have worked with people from the multinational's headquarters or another firm, who may be suitable job candidates. Patriates are likely to have business and social contacts with competent individuals available for present and future positions. Employees at the host site or with international experience may be in a better position to recruit individuals than the human resource managers in the home office. Some individuals are reluctant to work for a foreign-owned company because they believe they will not receive the same consideration as a national of the parent company. Patriates may believe they are being passed over for those favored by headquarters. Having patriates act as internal and external recruiters and coaches, as described earlier in this paper, would serve to alleviate some of these concerns and encourage qualified patriates and other individuals to apply for various positions.

Selection

Although an individual's manager, peers and subordinates may be consulted, the decision about whom to send on an international assignment is often made by top managers who may be the most removed from the situation (Snow, Davison, Snell & Hambrick, 1996). Some companies look for individuals with a connection to the host country through ancestry, education in that country and/or its culture, and prior work experience. Although the major reason for expatriate difficulty and failure is "lack of suitability" (Klaus, 1995) based on the characteristics of the individual expatriate, many companies do not adequately use a comprehensive process that includes the individual's and organization's needs (Harvey, 1996). The expatriate may have never visited the location of his/her new assignment nor met new coworkers before starting. Only 60% of companies offer a previsit orientation of two or three days for the expatriate to become familiar with the new country and facility (Solomon, 1995). Whether in person or via teleconference, patriates should participate in interviewing the potential expatriate. Lack of consultation with the patriates sends a signal that their concerns and opinions are not important. It may create resentment and a lack of interest in helping the expatriate. Patriates may be a valuable source of information about the "fit" of expatriate candidates with the work groups in a particular locale.

Training

Much of what has been written on international assignments centers on preparing the expatriate for the new country. Training host country nationals should also be part of this preparation. Vance and Paderon (1993) argue that it is morally appropriate to prepare and train the host country workforce for the incoming expatriate. According to them, this humanistic concern would assist the process of expatriate adjustment and performance and build the cross-cultural skills of the patriates. Such training can take place on-site at the host country facility. Alternatively, host country nationals can be trained at the company's headquarters (Solomon, 1993). U. S. firms, which employ the largest number of expatriates, are sending foreign patriates to the U.S. for training in a variety of skill areas and to familiarize them with the corporate culture. There is little recognition of the valuable role host country nationals play in the successful training of the visiting patriate and the long term psycho-social benefits that could be gained. In general, cultural training is more effective when using intercultural interactions (Shay & Tracey, 1997) which are more realistic when a patriate participates. Both the expatriate and patriate learn in such instances and the company transmits its appreciation of cross-cultural awareness.

Compensation

The information available about international compensation is often concerned with practical issues such as change in a certain standard of living and tax consequences. While these are important, the approach we take is to involve patriates in international assignments by linking part of their compensation to the success of the expatriate in their group. Employers commonly offer premium pay for foreign assignments to cover differences in cost of living and as an incentive to go to some locations (Latta, 1998). Similarly, employers should reward those patriates who are actively involved with helping the expatriate become acculturated to a new country. Patriates designated as coaches should receive some form of direct or indirect compensation for the extra time devoted to assisting the expatriate, especially if it is expended outside of working hours. The social credit and contributions to culture-building by patriates should be recognized by the organization.

FINAL NOTE

It has been the theme of this paper that employees of the host country facility are a social resource that can facilitate the expatriation process. We believe patriates are an untapped resource in offering valuable input into international human resource decisions. The recommendations we offer have the potential for a high yield to the organization and a positive experience for both the expatriate as well as host country nationals. This should be evident in more successful expatriate assignments and easier expatriate spouse and family adjustment to a different environment. As suggested throughout the paper, additional benefits that accrue through patriate involvement may be better communication among personnel in the host country facility and headquarters, more fully utilized patriate talent, greater expatriate and patriate commitment to the organization, and reduced costs of expatriation.

REFERENCES

Aldrich, H.E. (1979). *Organizations and environments*. Englewood Cliffs: Prentice-Hall, Inc.

Antal, A.B. (1993). Organizational change in multinational corporations. *Management Development Review*, 6: 24-32.

Are you entitled to paybacks? (1998, March). Global HR news, *HR Focus*, 75, S5.

Arthur, M.B. & Rousseau, D.M. (1996). *The boundaryless career: A new employment principle for a new organizational era.* New York: Oxford University Press.

Barton, R & Bishko, M. (1998, March). Global mobility strategy. *HR Focus,* 75 (3), S7-S8.

Benchmarking for placement. (1998, March). *HR Focus,* 75 (3), S5.

Birdseye, M.G., & Hill, J.S. (1995). Individual-organizational/work and environmental influences on expatriate turnover tendencies: An empirical study. *Journal of International Business Studies,* 23 (4), 787-813.

Black, J.S. & Gregersen, H.B. (1992, Summer). Serving two masters: Managing the dual allegiance of expatriate employees. *Sloan Management Review,* 33, 61-71.

Burt, R.S. (1992). *The social structure of competition.* Boston: Harvard University Press.

Clark, C.C. & Lipp, G.D. (1998). Conflict resolution for contrasting cultures. *Training and Development,* 52 (2): 20-33.

Dolainski, S. (1997, February). Are expats getting lost in the translation? *Workforce,* 2 (1), 32-39.

Don't be an ugly American manager. (1995, October 16). *Fortune,* 132 (8), 225.

Feldman, D.C. & Bolin, M.C. (1997). The impact of on-site mentoring on expatriate socialization: A structural equation modeling approach. In M. Schnake & S.H. Barr (Eds.), 1997 *Proceedings of the Southern Management Association,* 170-172.

Fitzgerald-Turner, B. (1997, June). International agenda: Myths of expatriate life. *HR Magazine,* 42 (6), 65-74.

Frazee, V. (1998, May). Send your expats prepared for success. *Workforce,* 77 (5) (Global Suppl.), 15-22.

Gates, S. (1996, July/August). Research roundup: Managing expatriates' expectations. *Across the Board,* 33, p. 58.

Globokar, T. (1996). Intercultural management in Eastern Europe: an empirical study of a French-Slovenian plant. *International Studies of Management & Organization,* 26 (3): 47-60.

Groh, K. & Allen, M. (1998, March). Global staffing: Are expatriates the only answer? *HR Focus Special Report on Expatriate Management,* 75 (3), S1-S2.

Harvey, M. (1996). The selection of managers for foreign assignments: A planning perspective. *Columbia Journal of World Business,* 31, 102-118.

Hofstede, G. (1991). *Cultures and organizations: Software of the mind.* London: McGraw-Hill, Inc.

Ibarra, H. (1992). Structural alignments, individual strategies, and managerial action: Elements toward a network theory of getting things done. In N. Nohria & R.G. Eccles (Eds.), *Networks and organizations: Structure, form, and actions* (pp. 165-188). Boston: Harvard Business School Press.

Katz, J.P. & Siefer, D.M. (1996). It's a different world out there: Planning for expatriate success through selection, pre-departure training and on-site socialization. *Human Resource Planning,* 19, 32-47.

Klaus, K.J. (1995, Spring). How to establish an effective expatriate program. *Employment Relations Today,* 22 (1), 59-70.

Knoke D., & Burt, R.S. (1983). Prominence. In R.S. Burt, M.J. Minor & Associates

(Eds.), *Applied network analysis: A methodological introduction* (pp. 195-220). Beverly Hills: Sage Publications, Inc.

Knoke, D., & Kuklinski, J. (1982). *Network analysis.* Beverly Hills: Sage Publications.

Labianca, G., & Brass, D.J., & Gray, B. (1998). Social networks and perceptions of intergroup conflict: The role of negative relationships and third parties. *The Academy of Management Journal,* 41 (1), 55-67.

Latta, G.W. (1998, March). Expatriate incentives: Beyond tradition. *HR Focus Special Report on Expatriate Management,* 75, S3-S4.

Lilly prepares its people to take on the world. (1996, January). *Personnel Journal,* 75, 58.

Mervosh, E.M. & McClenahen, J.S. (1997, Dec. 1). The care and feeding of expats. *Industry Week,* 22, 68-72.

Odenwald, S. (1996). Global work teams. *Training and Development Journal,* 50 (2), 54-58.

Pfeffer, J. (1983). Organizational demography. In L. Cummings & B. Staw (Eds.), *Research in organizational behavior* (vol. 5, pp. 299-357). Greenwich: JAI Press.

Ralston, D., Terpstra, R., Cunniff, M., & Gustafson, D. (1995). Do expatriates change their behavior to fit a foreign culture? A study of American expatriates, strategies of upward influence. *Management International Review,* 35, 109-122.

Scott, J. (1991). *Social network analysis: A handbook.* London: Sage Publications Ltd.

Shay, J.P. & Tracey, J.B. (1997). Expatriate managers: Reasons for failure and implications for training. *Cornell Hotel and Restaurant Administration Quarterly,* February, 30-39.

Sievers, C. (1998, March). Work/Family: Key to a successful assignment. *HR Focus Special Report on Expatriate Management,* 75 (3), S9-S10.

Snow, C.C., Davison, S.C. Snell, S.A. & Hambrick, D.C. (1996). Use transnational teams to globalize your company. *Organizational Dynamics,* 24 (4), 50-68.

Solomon, C.M. (1995, November). HR's helping hand pulls global inpatriates on board. *Personnel Journal,* 74, 40-49.

Solomon, C. M. (1993, October). Transplanting corporate culture globally. *Personnel Journal,* 72, 78-88.

Takeuchi, R. (1997). *Expatriate success and failure revisited: a taxonomy and consequences of international assignment outcomes.* Paper presented at the annual meeting of the Academy of Management, Boston, MA.

Tichy, N.M., Tushman, M.L., & Fombrun, C. (1979). Social network analysis for organizations. *Academy of Management Review,* 4 (4): 507-519.

Tung, R. (1987, May). Expatriate assignments: enhancing success and minimizing failure. *Academy of Management Executive,* 1 (2), 117-125.

Vance, C.M. & Paderon, E.S. (1993). An ethical argument for host country workforce training and development in the expatriate management assignment. *Journal of Business Ethics,* 12: 635-641.

Wagner, W.G., Pfeffer J. & O'Reilly, C.A., III. (1984). Organizational demography and turnover in top management groups. *Administrative Science Quarterly,* 29, 74-92.

Human Resources Management Practices in China: Township and Village Enterprises versus Sino-Foreign Joint Ventures

Zhen Xiong Chen
Jiing-Lih Farh

SUMMARY. Based on a survey of 308 firms in China, this paper compares the human resource management practices of Township and Village Enterprises (TVEs) with the Sino-foreign joint ventures (SFJVs) formed between TVEs and foreign firms. Systematic differences in employment practices are found in recruiting, educational qualifications of top management, training, benefits, and the role of unions in enterprise management. These differences are consistent with the predictions of institutional theory. Results are discussed in terms of implications for future research and management of enterprises in China. *[Article copies available for a fee from The Haworth Document Delivery Service: 1-800-342-9678. E-mail address: getinfo@haworthpressinc.com <Website: http://www.haworthpressinc.com>]*

KEYWORDS. Human resources management practices, institutional theory, township and village enterprises, Sino-foreign joint ventures, China

---

Zhen Xiong Chen is Assistant Professor, School of Business, Hong Kong Baptist University, Hong Kong (E-mail: georgezx@hkbu.edu.hk).

Jiing-Lih Farh is affiliated with the Department of Management of Organizations, Hong Kong University of Science and Technology (E-mail: mnlfarh@usthk.ust.hk).

[Haworth co-indexing entry note]: "Human Resources Management Practices in China: Township and Village Enterprises versus Sino-Foreign Joint Ventures." Chen, Zhen Xiong, and Jiing-Lih Farh. Co-published simultaneously in *Journal of Transnational Management Development* (International Business Press, an imprint of The Haworth Press, Inc.) Vol. 4, No. 3/4, 1999, pp. 45-65; and: *Culture and International Business* (ed: Kip Becker) International Business Press, an imprint of The Haworth Press, Inc., 2000, pp. 45-65. Single or multiple copies of this article are available for a fee from The Haworth Document Delivery Service [1-800-342-9678, 9:00 a.m. - 5:00 p.m. (EST). E-mail address: getinfo@haworthpressinc.com].

45

INTRODUCTION

Since 1979, two new types of enterprises have been booming in China: one is township and village enterprises (TVEs) and the other is Sino-foreign joint ventures (SFJVs). At present, these two types of enterprises have become important forces in China's economy in addition to state-owned enterprises. Due to the differences of ownership and institutional environments of these two types of enterprises, their human resources management (HRM) practices are varied. These differences can be explained from the perspective of institutional theory.

In the current study, we examined variations in HRM practices between TVEs and SFJVs. The purposes of the study are twofold. First, by contrasting the HRM practices of these two new, albeit important, forms of organizations, we hope to contribute to a better understanding of the human resource management practices in China. Second, we sought to determine if institutional theory, a product of Western organization theories, could account for variations in HRM practices in these two types of firms in China. By conducting this research, we hope to shed light on the culture-boundness of Western institutional theory in an eastern context.

Township and Village Enterprises and Sino-Foreign Joint Ventures: A Brief Introduction

Since 1949, the model form of industrial enterprises in communist China has been state-owned (and operated) enterprises (SOEs). Until 1979, the state government strictly restricted the development of TVEs, those that are owned and operated by people in towns and villages in rural China, and consequently they constituted a small, nonsignificant sector of the economy. In 1978 China began its economic reform of the agricultural sector. The ensuing increase in agricultural productivity released tens of millions of surplus peasant laborers into local job markets. To address the need for employment opportunities and the development of consumer goods industries, the government began to encourage the development of collective rural enterprises in 1979. Since then, the growth of TVEs has been nothing but spectacular. By the end of 1996, there were 23.36 million TVEs with 135.83 million employees; the gross industrial output value of collectively owned TVEs in the year of 1996 was RMB 276.3 billion yuan (*China Statistical Yearbook*, 1997). With the steady decline of the state-owned sector,

TVEs were said to hold the key to China's economic future (Byrd & Lin, 1990; Chen & Chen, 1994).

Although individuals own some TVEs, the majority, especially the larger ones, is collectively owned by local citizens. The township and village governments are the representatives holding the property rights of TVEs. To improve performance, the local governments often entrust TVEs to private operators through an elastic contracting system (Chen, Zheng & Zhang, 1992). Therefore, TVEs have become a mixed property form, with local governments and private operators claiming property rights over them (Nee, 1992). Under partial reform in China, TVEs operate under two different economic systems simultaneously–a planning or redistributive economy and a market economy. Due to these reasons, TVEs are considered as a "hybrid" form of organization in China. Since TVEs are not owned by the state, they are unfettered by state bureaucracy and enjoy considerable autonomy in day-to-day operations, including deciding on their own HRM practices.

Like TVEs, Sino-foreign joint ventures (SFJVs) are a relatively new form of organization in China. Prior to 1979, foreign direct investments were not allowed in China. With the introduction of market reform and the open door policy, foreign investors rushed to China to tap its huge market potential and vast human resources. By the end of 1996, there were 240,447 registered foreign direct investment enterprises in China with a total investment of U.S. $715.32 billion (*China Statistical Yearbook*, 1997). Among the different modes of entry into China's market, Sino-foreign joint ventures are very popular (Beamish, 1993). In these joint ventures, foreign partners often inject capital, provide management and technology know-how, and are responsible for marketing the products in international markets, whereas Chinese partners provide land, labor, factory facilities, public relations, and access to the domestic market. So far, the largest group of foreign direct investment in China has come from overseas Chinese communities (especially from Hong Kong) with the remainder mainly coming from Western countries and Japan.

In this study, we apply institutional theory to contrast the differences of HRM practices between TVEs and SFJVs. The key points of institutional theory and its relationship with HRM are summarized as follows.

Institutional Theory and Its Link with Human Resource Management

Evolving from organization theories since the mid-1970s (Meyer & Rowan, 1977; Scott, 1987; Zucker, 1987), institutional theory has recently been employed to explain differences in human resource management practices across firms (Wright & McMahan, 1992). The ideas of institutionalism provide researchers in human resource management (HRM) with a new perspective that is different from other more established approaches (e.g., agency theory, strategic human resource management).

Institutional theory provides a rich, complex view of organizations (Zucker, 1987). It "focuses on organizational conformity with social rules and rituals. It is a perspective concerned more with legitimacy than efficiency" (Orru, Biggart, & Hamilton, 1991). From an institutional perspective, many structures, programs, and practices in organizations, attain legitimacy through the social construction of reality (Wright & McMahan, 1992). Organizations that fit the institutionalized environment are found to be more legitimate, potentially more successful, and more likely to survive (Meyer & Rowan, 1983).

One of the key assumptions behind the institutional perspective is that some organizational structures and practices–rational or irrational, efficient or inefficient–may be accepted and adopted by organizations without question, or taken for granted (Scott, 1987). From an institutional perspective, a given practice may serve some function, yet this fact does not necessarily prove that the need fulfilled is the basis for the practices' origin.

There are many ways in which organizational structures and practices can become institutionalized. For example, some practices may be derived from cultural values, industrial tradition, firm history, and popular management folklore (Eisenhardt, 1988). Other practices can be imposed coercively, as in the case of government mandating laws or companies mandating changes in an acquired subsidiary. Still, some other practices can be induced through outside agents providing rewards to organizations that confirm with the wishes of the agents. Finally, practices can be acquired through one organization modeling its practices based on practices of other organizations as a means to appear legitimate or up-to-date (DiMaggio & Powell, 1983; Scott, 1987; Wright & McMahan, 1992).

Even though many studies on institutional practices have focused on the institutionalization of organizational structure (Scott, 1987), Wright and McMahan (1992) argued that some of the institutional influences can be found in HRM. They proposed that "many HRM practices may be the results of social construction processes whereby external entities influence the creation and implementation of practices that come to attain a mythical sense of legitimacy" (p. 314). Institutional theory thus may provide explanation for why HRM practices vary between different types of enterprises.

HYPOTHESES

Although both TVEs and SFJVs operate in China, they are faced with different institutional constraints. TVEs are indigenous Chinese organizations owned and operated by the local Chinese. Their employment practices are likely to conform to the prevailing Chinese social norms and shaped heavily by what are considered to be "legitimate" practices in China. As noted above, the state-owned enterprise is the dominant form of industrial organization in China. Many of its HRM practices (e.g., cradle-to-grave care systems for employees, egalitarian reward systems) have become ingrained in the collective mind of the Chinese people. These practices are taken for granted by both Chinese managers and employees.

The institutional environment facing SFJVs is quite different due to the influence of foreign ownership. In joint ventures, major business decisions are made by their boards of directors, which consist of both foreign and Chinese members. Since it is commonly believed in China that foreign management practices are superior to Chinese ones, Chinese partners are willing to yield to foreign partners on the management of the joint ventures. Consequently, the social norms and practices of the foreign partners heavily influence the HRM practices of SFJVs.

We therefore expect that the HRM practices of TVEs will conform to Chinese social norms and resemble those of SOEs whereas the HRM practices of SFJVs will conform to the social norms and practices of foreign partners. Specifically, we expect differences in sources of recruiting key personnel, in strategies to attract and retain key personnel, in methods to motivate employees, and in the role of unions in enterprise management.

Sources of Key Personnel

Key personnel are the managerial and technical staff critical to the success of enterprise. In traditional Chinese societies, personal connections or relations (known as *guanxi* in Chinese), built around kinship and locality, were important features of Chinese social relations. When the Communists took over China in 1949, they began a series of campaigns and movements to transform traditional particularistic values such as *guanxi* to universalistic socialist values such as comradeship (Vogel, 1965). As this gigantic project of value transformation was achieved largely through fear, it lost its effectiveness quickly when the Party started to loosen administrative control over people's daily lives in late 1970s. With the resurgence of market utilitarianism and the limited institutionalization of laws and administrative regulations, traditional social norms such as *guanxi* and *renqing* (i.e., interpersonal favors and generosity) have returned to China with a vengeance. "Walking through the back door" (i.e., using personal networks for illicit gain or bypassing the bureaucracy) is widely known to be the most effective and necessary means to get things done in today's communist China (Chu & Ju, 1990; King, 1991).

On what basis is *guanxi* formed in Chinese contexts? Recent research indicated that *guanxi* is often built on shared attributes including locality (i.e., same native origin), kinship, common surname, common dialect, past associations (e.g., teacher-student, classmate, co-worker), etc. (Farh, Tsui, & Cheng, 1995). While these shared attributes or backgrounds do not predispose good *guanxi,* individuals who do not share them will have fewer bases on which to build personal relationships than individuals who do.

To the extent that social norms of *guanxi* influence TVEs, the recruitment policies of TVEs are likely to favor local people (as opposed to outsiders), who tend to have more *guanxi* bases with the town and village officials. We therefore expect that TVEs will tend to recruit key personnel from local sources instead of from a broader region. Due to this parochial recruiting policy and the general lower level of education in the Chinese countryside, we expect that the level of education of top management in TVEs will be lower than in SFJVs. To counter the disadvantages of hiring key personnel from local sources (which inevitably results in a shallow pool of talent), TVEs are more likely to invest heavily in training.

The situation differs for joint ventures. When foreign firms establish joint ventures in China, they have little affinity toward the people of a particular locality. In addition, foreign firms, whether they are from Hong Kong or the U.S., operate by the logic of the market economy; that is, they tend to put a stronger emphasis on objective qualifications than on personal connections in recruiting and selection. To the extent that foreign partners influence SFJVs, they tend to recruit key personnel from a broader labor market. Because qualifications and skills are the bases for recruitment, SFJVs should have less need to invest in training of key personnel, and the level of education of its top management is likely to be higher. From the above, we propose the following hypothesis:

H1: *In comparison with SFJVs, TVEs are more likely to recruit key personnel from local areas, provide more in-house and outside training to employees, and their top management will have lower levels of educational qualifications.*

Strategy to Attract and Retain Key Personnel

Offering comprehensive benefits with low salary has been a standard employment practice in China's state-owned firms (Walder, 1983). The benefits offered are so comprehensive that they often make firms in socialist countries (e.g., Scandinavian) pale by comparison. SOEs typically provide employees with free meals, housing, hospitalization, schooling for their children, bus transportation to and from work, haircuts, recreational facilities, jobs for the dependents, etc. While benefits are comprehensive, salary differentials across ranks are compressed due to the Communist's egalitarian ideology. For example, Hay, Morris, Lui, and Yao (1994) reported that the average salary received by the top managers in China's SOEs was only 1.36 times of that of workers in 1987 (although top managers had perquisites such as cars, better housing, and expense accounts unavailable to ordinary workers). Consistent with the social norms in China, TVEs are likely to offer high benefits with low salary to attract and retain key personnel. Actually, a case study conducted by Wong, Liu, Liu, and Shi (1994) has provided some evidence for this assumption, which reported that some TVEs did provide senior managers and technicians with free housing.

Under the influence of foreign firms, SFJVs are more likely to offer a high salary with low benefit approach (Tang, Lai, Cheng, & Chang, 1996). This is especially true for foreign firms coming from Hong

Kong or Taiwan. Empirical studies have shown that firms in these economies offered meager benefits for their employees but gave large bonuses because employees prefer cash to benefits, and there are few vigorously enforced employment laws that mandate benefits to employees (Farh, 1995; Tang, 1989). For example, as of 1996, Hong Kong does not have laws that require private employers to provide employees with pensions. Based on the above reasoning, we propose the following hypothesis:

H2: *As compared with SFJVs, TVEs are more likely to use a high benefits with low salary approach to attract and retain key personnel.*

Motivating Employees

There are two broad categories of rewards for motivating employees: monetary (including salary and benefits) and non-monetary (e.g., job enrichment, participating in management, employee relations and advancement, etc.). Traditionally, Chinese SOEs have relied heavily on non-monetary rewards to motivate employees including worker participation in decision making, citations for merit, orders of commendation, and honorable titles, e.g., model worker, while tangible rewards were greatly neglected (Chan, 1990; Martinko & Yang, 1990; Tung, 1981; Zhu & Dowling, 1994). To the extent that these practices are followed, we expect that TVEs are less likely to rely on monetary rewards to motivate their employees.

In contrast to China, monetary rewards are deemed very important in Hong Kong, Taiwan, and Western countries where most of foreign parent firms of SFJVs come from (Redding, 1990; Farh, 1995). Therefore, we propose the following hypothesis to be tested:

H3: *TVEs are more likely to use non-monetary incentives to motivate employees than SFJVs.*

Union Participation

Under communist ideology, worker unions along with the Party and the enterprise administration form the core of enterprise leadership. Thus, unions in SOEs are entitled to participate in all major business decisions (Nyaw, 1994). For instance, a survey conducted by the Chinese Academy of Social Sciences (CASS), in which the data from 400 of the larger SOEs covering the year 1980-1987 were collected, indicated that about 70% of the firms allowed workers to participate in major decisions, including wage/bonus decisions, assignment of workers to posts, and capital investment (Hay, Morris, Liu, and Yao, 1994). Following this tradition, TVEs are more likely to have union participation in major business decisions. A case study conducted by Ding (1994) provided evidence for this argument. Ding reported that a union in a typical TVE participated the following major decisions: long term planning of the company; the adjustment of the schemes of wages and bonus for the employees; the training plan for the employees; and the use of welfare funds of the company.

The situation is different for SFJVs. In Taiwan, the ROC government adopted a policy that placed organized labor under strict government control for nearly four decades (from the 1950s to the 1980s) (Farh, 1995). Taiwanese workers were not allowed to strike until martial law was lifted in 1987. In Hong Kong, the union movement is also weak (Farh, Leung, & Tse, 1995). An outstanding feature of its labor relations is the low level of industrial conflict. Between 1987 and 1991, the average number of working days lost to worker protests per 1,000 wage earners and salaried employees per year was just one, one of the lowest averages in the world (Labor Department of Hong Kong Government, 1992). In the U.S., union representation has had a steady decline since the 1950s. This decline has accelerated since the early 1980s due to global economy, shifting industry structures, and employer resistance (Milkovich & Boudreau, 1994). Unions in these countries are generally considered adversaries of management or shareholder interests, and should be kept at bay if at all possible. Influenced by foreign partners who view unions as adversaries, SFJVs are less likely to involve unions in major business decisions. Drawing from the above arguments, we propose the following hypothesis:

H4: *Unions in TVEs are more likely to participate in major business decisions than those in SFJVs.*

METHOD

Sample

The data used for this study came from a survey of TVEs in the Pearl River Delta (PRD) of the Guangdong Province of South China.

The survey was jointly conducted by the Research Center of the PRD Economic Development and Management of Sun Yat-Sen University in Guangzhou, PRC. The PRD region was an ideal place for studying TVEs for two reasons. First, being adjacent to Hong Kong, the PRD is one of the fastest growing regions in China, and much of that growth has been attributed to local TVEs. Second, the PRD region has a large concentration of Sino-foreign joint ventures in China, many of which were formed by TVEs and firms from Hong Kong.

A total of 1,000 collective TVEs and their joint ventures were sampled in the survey. To ensure the representativeness of the sample, a stratified sampling plan was followed based on geographic region (city/county) and firm size. Samples were drawn equally from small-size firms (number of employees under 200), mid-size firms (200-500), and large firms (over 500). Surveys were mailed to the Chinese general managers of each company. Only surveys with complete information regarding the respondent were included in the study.

Altogether, we got 308 usable questionnaires for a response rate of 31%. In terms of the type of enterprise surveyed, 229 (74%) were collective TVEs, 44 (14%) were equity joint ventures formed between collective TVEs and foreign firms, 13 (4%) were contractual joint ventures formed between TVEs and foreign firms, and 3 were unknown. This particular study's sample consisted of the 229 collective TVEs and the 44 Sino-foreign equity joint ventures. Among the joint ventures, most of their foreign parents were companies from Hong Kong (88%) with the remaining from Taiwan, Japan, and the U.S. Since the size distribution of the sample matched that of the sampling population, the sample seemed to be representative.

Measures

Sources of Key Personnel. In this study the term key personnel refers to managerial and technical employees. We asked the executives: (1) if they recruited key personnel from local area only or also from other regions; (2) if their company had in-house programs to train key personnel. Both questions were measured using a "yes or no" format. In addition, the executives were asked to estimate the number of employees their companies sent for outside training in the past 12 months. The level of education of top management (defined as general manager or deputy general manager) was measured by asking the respondents to indicate their level of formal education (i.e., primary school or below, junior high school, high school, college and above).

Strategy to Attract and Retain Key Personnel. We asked the executives to indicate if their company used high salary as a means to attract and retain key personnel. We also inquired if their companies offered three major types of benefits: employee housing, job placement assistance for a spouse, and job/school placement assistance for children. All questions were answered in a "yes or no" format. Since the three benefit items were moderately correlated (Alpha = .70), they were first standardized and then combined to form a composite benefit measure.

Method to Motivate Employees. We asked the executives to indicate the most effective way to motivate employees. The response options included wage and benefit, employee relations, job enrichment, and participative management. Their responses were coded as 1 for wage and benefit, and 0 for all others.

Union Participation. We asked the executives about the role that the union played in their companies. Their responses were coded as 1 for the union participating in major business decisions, and 0 for the union participating in employee welfare matters only such as organizing welfare committee and recreation activities.

Controls. Since human resource management practices may vary depending on the type of industry, the size of the company, and the newness of the company, these three variables were incorporated as controls in this study. Industry was dummy coded (1 = consumer goods, 0 = industrial goods). Size was measured by the number of full-time employees employed. The newness of the company was measured by the stage of establishment (1 = before 1979, 2 = 1979-1983, 3 = 1984-1988, and 4 = 1989 and later). We divide the stages of establishment of TVEs and SFJVs based on the following reasons: stage 1 (before 1979) was the period before China started its economic reform; stage 2 (1979-1983) was the early development period of China's economic reform; stage 3 (1984-1988) was the "golden stage of economic reform" in China; stage 4 (1989 and later) was the period after the "June 4" Tiananmen Event.

Data Analysis Strategy

The dependent variables of this study are human resource practices, some of which are continuous and others are dichotomous measures. We used OLS regression to examine the effect of enterprise type (TVE versus SFJV) on continuous HRM practice measures. In the case of dichotomous dependent measures, OLS regression is inappropriate since key assumptions underlying the technique are violated, which can produce biased and invalid regression coefficients. For these dependent measures, we performed logistic regression, which resolves the problems by modeling a linear relationship between a set of predictor variables and the logarithmic odds of a dichotomous dependent variables. In both types of regression analysis, we controlled for differences in industry type, stage of establishment, and size. The above hypotheses can be tested by examining if the beta coefficient for enterprise type was significant for each of the HRM practices in the logistic or OLS regression models.

RESULTS

Type of Enterprise and Sample Characteristics

Table 1 presents the frequency distribution and chi-square tests of size, industry type, and position of the respondents by type of enterprise. Several interesting findings are revealed from the table. First, size was unrelated to type of enterprise. There was a relatively even distribution of small, medium, and large size firms in each type of enterprise. Second, industry type was significantly related to type of enterprise, as there was a higher concentration of joint ventures in the consumer goods industry than TVEs (66% versus 44%). Finally, there was no significant difference between TVEs and SFJVs in terms of the respondent's position. Overall, 75% of the respondents were general managers or deputy general managers; only 25% of the respondents were middle level managers.

Table 2 provides the frequency distribution, means, and standard deviations for the dependent measures by type of enterprise. We shall refer to these results when we interpret the findings of the regression analysis.

Test of Hypotheses

H1 (Sources of Key Personnel). The results of the regression analyses are presented in Table 3. As can be seen from Table 3, the type of

TABLE 1. Sample Characteristics: Township and Village Enterprises versus Sino-Foreign Joint Ventures

	Town & Village		Joint Venture		
	N	%	N	%	Chi-square
Size					.4
Under 200	73	32.4	14	32.6	
200-500	88	39.1	15	34.9	
500 and above	64	28.4	14	32.6	
Industry Type[1]					7.4*
Consumer goods	100	43.7	29	65.9	
Industrial goods	129	56.3	15	34.1	
Position of Respondent					.5
General manager	124	59.0	20	55.6	
Deputy general manager	31	14.8	7	19.4	
Middle level manager	55	26.2	9	25.0	

Note 1: Consumer goods industries include household appliances, furniture, clothing, shoes, foods and drinks, toys etc.; Industrial goods industries include building materials, metals, chemicals, leather, plastics, paper, packaging materials and medicine, etc.
*p < .05 (two-tailed)

enterprise had a significant effect on recruitment source, in-house development, outside training, and top management education. These results can be interpreted by examining the descriptive statistics presented in Table 2. As hypothesized, SFJVs were more likely to recruit key personnel from other regions than were TVEs (70.7% vs. 49.6%). SFJVs were less likely to offer in-house development programs (78% vs. 92%) and sent fewer personnel out for outside training (16.5 vs. 38.2 employees per company each year) than TVEs. Moreover, the top management personnel of SFJVs tended to be better educated than those of TVEs (81.5% vs. 54.8% with high school or above degrees). Thus, H1 was strongly supported.

H2 (Method to Attract and Retain Key Personnel). Two major types of strategies to attract and retain key personnel were compared in this

TABLE 2. Human Resource Management Practices by Types of Enterprises

Human Resource Management Practices	Town and Village		Joint Venture	
	Frequency	**Percentage**	**Frequency**	**Percentage**
Recruitment source				
Local and other regions	111	49.6	29	70.7
Local only	113	50.4	12	29.3
In-house development				
Yes	206	92.0	32	78.0
No	18	8.0	9	22.0
Top management education				
Junior high school or below	70	45.2	5	18.5
High school	71	45.8	17	63.0
College and above	14	9.0	5	18.5
High salary to attract or retain				
Yes	97	51.6	29	67.4
No	91	48.4	14	32.6
Employee housing				
Yes	73	38.8	9	20.9
No	115	61.2	34	79.1
Placement for spouse				
Yes	36	19.1	4	9.3
No	152	80.9	39	90.7
Placement for children				
Yes	31	16.5	1	2.3
No	157	83.5	42	97.7
Method to Motivate Employees				
Wage and benefits	145	69.4	27	65.9
Other methods	64	30.6	14	34.1
Union participation				
Major decisions	74	40.7	8	22.9
Employee welfare decisions only	108	59.3	27	77.1
	Mean	**SD**	**Mean**	**SD**
Outside training (number of employees sent out)	38.2	73.9	16.5	21.7

TABLE 3. Logistic and OLS Regression Analyses on HRM Practices[a]

| | | Control Variables | | Size | Type of enterprise | |
| | | Industry | Stage | | | |
	Intercept	**B**	**B**	**B**	**B**	**Model Statistics**[b]
Sources of Key Personnel						
Recruitment source (0 = local, 1 = other)	−.46 (.36)	−.31 (.28)	.06 (.14)	.01** (.00)	.79** (.41)	15.27**
In-house development (0 = no, 1 = yes)	2.99** (.66)	.52 (.46)	−.35 (.24)	−.00 (.00)	−1.01* (.51)	9.84*
Outside training (no. of employees)	14.61 (10.49)	−3.15 (8.32)	2.93 (4.20)	.038* (.009)	−24.19** (12.22)	.09**
Top management education	1.74** (.14)	.00 (.10)	−.013 (.05)	.00 (.00)	.37** (.15)	.05°
Attract & Retain Key Personnel						
High salary (0 = no, 1 = yes)	−.63 (.39)	.32 (.30)	.33* (.15)	−.00 (.00)	.43 (.40)	12.32*
Employee housing (0 = no, 1 = yes)	−.07 (.39)	−.62* (.31)	−.16 (.15)	.00 (.00)	−.62° (.44)	11.96*
Placement for spouse (0 = no, 1 = yes)	−1.59** (.49)	.04 (.38)	.02 (.19)	.00 (.00)	−.89° (−.59)	3.37
Placement for children (0 = no, 1 = yes)	−2.13** (.56)	.02 (.41)	.15 (.21)	.00 (.00)	−2.30* (1.05)	9.86*
Method to Motivate Employees (0 = others, 1 = wages & benefits)	.64 (.39)	.33 (.30)	.04 (.15)	−.00 (.00)	−.23 (.41)	1.49
Union Participation (0 = welfare only, 1 = major decisions)	−.17 (.39)	−.11 (.32)	−.04 (.16)	−.00 (.00)	−.87* (.48)	5.51

[a]Standard errors are in parentheses. Coding scheme for independent variables are as follows: Type of Enterprise (0 = township and village, 1= joint venture); Industry (0 = industrial, 1 = consumer); Stage (1 = before 1979, 2 = 1979-83, 3 = 1984-88, 4 = after 1989).
[b]The model statistics are a global chi-square for logistic regression and R^2 for the OLS regression.
°$p < .10$, * $p < .05$, **$p < .01$ (one-tailed test for Type of Enterprise, two-tailed tests for control variables)

study: salary and benefits. Hypothesis 2 predicts that in comparison with TVEs, SFJVs are more likely to use high salary and low benefit strategies to attract and retain key personnel. The results of the regression analyses indicate that contrary to H2, there was no significant difference between TVEs and SFJVs in their likelihood of using a high-salary strategy. Among the control variables, the stage of establishment had a significant impact on the likelihood of a company to adopt a high-salary strategy, suggesting that newly founded firms were more likely to use a high-salary strategy to attract and retain key personnel than more established firms.

The percentages of three types of benefits offered in TVEs and SFJVs were compared across the two types of firms: employer provided housing, placement assistance for spouse and placement assistance for children. Results of logistic regression indicate that type of enterprise had a significant effect on placement assistance for children, and a marginally significant effect ($p < .10$) on employee housing and placement assistance for spouse (see Table 3). Table 2 provides the breakdown of benefits by type of enterprise. Consistent with H2, TVEs are more likely to offer housing to employees (39% vs. 21%), placement assistance for employee's spouses (19% vs. 9%), and placement assistance for employee's children (17% vs. 2%). Thus, H2 was partially supported.

H3 (Method to Motivate Employees). It was hypothesized that TVEs are more likely to use non-monetary incentives to motivate employees than SFJVs. Results of logistic regression analysis showed that there was no significant difference between TVEs and SFJVs in method of motivation. H3 was unsupported.

H4 (Union Role). It was hypothesized that unions in TVEs are more likely to participate in major business decisions than in SFJVs. The results of the regression analysis showed that type of enterprise had a significant effect on the role of union. As can be seen from Table 2, the percentage of TVEs in which unions participated in major business decisions was higher than that of SFJVs (41% vs. 23%). Thus, H4 was supported.

DISCUSSION AND CONCLUSION

Generally, the results of this study partially supported our hypotheses. Specifically, we found that the HRM practices of TVEs were systematically different from those of SFJVs in several important aspects: (1) they tended to recruit key personnel locally; (2) they were more willing to invest in training and development of their own key personnel; (3) they tended to fill top management positions with less educationally qualified individuals; (4) they were more likely to use generous benefit packages to attract and retain key personnel;

and (5) they were more likely to involve unions in major business decisions. All of the above were consistent with the general predictions of institutional theory, i.e., the HRM practices of TVEs are generally more consistent with the social norms in China than those of SFJVs. This suggests that institutional theory may be a valuable framework to understand variations in HRM practices of organizations in China. By understanding their unique institutional backgrounds, we can predict and explain differences in management practices across different types of firms in China. While emerging from a Western tradition, institutional theory seems to possess considerable, cross-cultural generality.

Somewhat surprising is the lack of support for H3 and only partial support for H2, both of which hypothesized that SFJVs should place a greater emphasis on monetary rewards in recruiting and motivating personnel than collective TVEs. Contrary to the predictions of institutional theory, both types of enterprises put equally strong emphasis on monetary incentives in recruiting and motivating employees. Given the Communist tradition of using non-material rewards to motivate employees while insisting on egalitarian pay for all, it is surprising to find that TVEs also depended heavily on wage and salary to retain, attract, and motivate employees. This suggests that the use of monetary rewards in recruiting and motivating employees in for-profit organizations may have attained full legitimacy in China.

Our speculation about changing social norms regarding financial rewards in China is corroborated by the findings of a recent study by Chen (1995). Comparing the reward allocation schemes preferred by Chinese employees (employed by Chinese state-owned enterprises) and U.S. employees, Chen found that the Chinese employees were more economically oriented than their US counterparts. Chinese employees preferred to invoke differential rules (those that result in unequal distribution of rewards) for the allocation of *both* material and socio-emotional rewards whereas their U.S. counterparts preferred a performance rule for the allocation of material rewards and equality rules for socio-emotional rewards. These results demonstrate that Chinese employees even in the state-owned enterprises have abandoned the old ideology of equality of outcomes for all. Under the mounting pressure of bankruptcy and layoffs in an increasingly competitive market-driven economy, productivity and efficiency have become the rules of the game. It is thus not surprising, after all, that the management of TVEs no longer follows the old traditions of SOEs and places exceedingly strong emphasis on monetary rewards as a major means to attract, motivate, and retain employees.

Furthermore, it is worth noting that stage, one of our control variables, had a significant positive effect on high salary to attract and retain key personnel. This suggests that TVEs and SFJVs that were founded more recently were more likely to use a high salary policy to attract and retain key personnel than those founded in an earlier period. As China moves away from a command economy to a market one, and her labor market turns freer over time, high salary policy becomes the predominant means for all firms to compete for human resources. Firms that were born in this period of time were imprinted with this ideology and thus more likely to pursue a high salary policy.

There are several important implications for foreign companies that are interested in operating in China. First, in looking for an indigenous Chinese firm as a partner in joint ventures, be prepared for marked differences in management practices. In this study, we compared TVEs with joint ventures formed between TVEs and foreign firms and found significant differences in management practices. Foreign firms that plan to form join ventures with Chinese state-owned firms are likely to find even bigger differences in management practices. Until these differences can be identified and neutralized, a clash of two management cultures is inevitable. Second, the following are areas in which management practices between foreign firms and indigenous Chinese firms are likely to occur: (a) should we hire people from our own local network or from a broad national labor market, (b) should we allow worker unions to be involved in major management decisions, (c) should we provide workers with broad or limited benefits, and (d) how important is education qualification for top management positions? Third, high salary policy and monetary incentive for performance are well accepted, probably expected, management practices in China. The by-products of a high salary policy (i.e., increasing labor costs and turnover) will be here to stay for some time to come. Foreign firms should be prepared to face the challenge of implementing effective incentive programs.

While the results are encouraging, they should be considered tentative due to several limitations. First, some of our measures are single items with a yes-no format. This inevitably increases the measurement error and reduces the statistical power of our tests. Therefore, our study is a conservative one. Second, the findings of this study were based on surveys provided by top management. To the extent that their responses were biased, the survey results might also be biased. Although previous research in the West has shown that top executives are reliable and valid informants of organizational practices (Philips, 1981), future research should use multiple methods to assess HRM practices. Finally, the majority of foreign partners of SFJVs in this study were from Hong Kong. Even though Hong Kong has a free market economy, and its social norms and business practices are very Western, it still shares common cultural roots with mainland China. Future studies should include joint ventures formed between Chinese firms and U.S. or European firms.

REFERENCES

Beamish, P.W.: The characteristics of joint ventures in the People's Republic of China, *Journal of International Marketing,* 1 (1993): 29-48.

Byrd, W.A. & Lin, Q.: *China's rural industry: structure, development and reform,* New York: Oxford University Press. 1990.

Chan, A.H.: Management reforms in China enterprises: the roadblocks that remain, in *Advances in Chinese Industrial Studies,* Vol.1 (part A), J. Child, J. & M. Lockett, ed., Jai Press Inc. 1990.

Chen, C.: New trends rewards allocation preferences: A Sino-US comparison, *Academy of Management Journal,* 38 (1995): 408-428.

Chen, Z.X. & Chen, W.X.: The development of township and village enterprises in China, in *The Trend of Economy of China in 1994,* P. K. Lau, ed., Hong Kong Commerce publisher. 1994. (in Chinese)

Chen, Z.X., Zheng, Z.C., & Zhang, X.J.: On the management mechanism of township and village enterprises in the Pearl Rive Delta in South China: Its advantages, contributing factors and revelations, in H. Q. Huang, ed.: *Economic Development of the Pearl River Delta: A Retrospect and Prospect* (pp. 221-232), Sun Yat-Sen University Press, Guangzhou, China. 1992. (In Chinese)

China Statistical Yearbook 1997. (In Chinese)

Chu, G.C. & Ju, Y.: *The Great Wall in Ruins–Communication and Cultural Change in China,* State University of New York Press. 1993.

Ding, Y.Z.: Fishing facility group company at town A, a case study, in *The investigations of China's township and village enterprises in 1990s,* R. Ma, J. Wong, H.S. Wong, & M. Yang, ed., Oxford University Press. 1994. (In Chinese)

DiMaggio, P.J. & Powell, W.W.: The iron cage revisited: Institutional isomorphism & collective rationality in organizational fields, in *The New Institutionalism in Organizational Analysis,* W.W. Powell & P.J. DiMaggio, ed., The University of Chicago Press. 1991. pp. 41-62.

Eisenhardt, K.: Agency-and institutional-theory explanations: The case of retail sales compensation, *Academy of Management Journal,* 31 (1988): 488-511.

Farh, J.L.: Human resource of management practices in Taiwan, in *Human Resource Management on the Pacific Rim: Institutions, Practices and Attitudes,* L.F. Moore & P.D. Jenning, ed., New York: De Gruyter. 1995. pp. 236-194.

Farh, J.L., Leung, K. & Tse, D.K.: Managing human resources in Hong Kong: 1997 and beyond. *The Columbia Journal of World Business,* (1995 summer): 53-59.

Farh, J.L., Tsui, A.S., & Cheng, B.S.: The Influence Of Relational Demography and *Guanxi:* The Chinese case, paper presented in the 1995 national meeting of the Academy of Management, Vancouver, Canada. 1995.

Hay, D., Marris, D., Liu, G., & Yao, S.: *Economic reform and state-owned enterprises in China, 1979-1987,* Clarendon Press, Oxford. 1994.

Huo, Y.P. & Glinow, M.A.V.: On transplanting human resource practices to China: A culture-driven approach, *International Journal of Manpower,* 16 (1995): 3-15.

King, A.Y.C.: Kuan-hsi and network building : A sociological interpretation, *Daedalus,* 120 (1991): 63-84.

Labor Department of Hong Kong Government: *Labor and Employment in Hong Kong.* 1992.

Martinko, M.J. & Yan, F.: A comparison of leadership theory and practices in the PRC and US, in Albert Nedd (eds): *International Human Resources Management Review,* 1 (1990): 109-122.

Meyer, J.W., & Rowan, B.: Institutional organizations: formal structure as myth and ceremony, *American Journal of Sociology,* 83 (1983): 340-363.

Milkovich, G.T., & Bondrean, J.W.: *Human resource management,* 7th ed., Richard D. Irwin, Inc. 1994.

Nee, V.: Organizational dynamics of market transition: Hybrid forms, property rights and mixed economy in China, *Administrative Science Quarterly,* 33 (1992): 11-27.

Nyaw, M.K.: Human resource management in the People's Republic of China, in *Human Resource Management in the Pacific Rim,* L. Moore and D. Jennings, ed., Berlin, New York: De Gruyter. 1994.

Orru, M., Biggart, N.M., & Hamilton, G.G.: Organizational isomorphism in East Asia, in *The New Institutionalism in Organizational Analysis,* W.W. Powell & P.J. DiMaggio, eds., The University of Chicago Press. 1991. pp. 316-319.

Redding, S.G.: *The spirit of Chinese capitalism,* New York: de Gruyter. 1990.

Scott, W.R.: The adolescence of institutional theory, *Administrative Science Quarterly,* 32 (1987): 493-511.

Tang, S.F.Y., Lai, E.W.K., Cheng, L.Z., & Zhang, S.Q.: Research report: Human resources management strategies and practices in foreign invested enterprises in the PRC, Hong Kong Institute of Human Resources Management and International Technologies and Economy Institute of Development Research center of the State Council, PRC. 1996.

Tung, R.L.: Patterns of motivation in Chinese industrial enterprises, *Academy of Management Review,* 6 (1981): 481-489.

Vogel, E.F.: From friendship to comradeship: The change in personal relationship in communist China, *The China Quarterly,* 21 (1965): 46-60.

Wong, H.S., Liu, S.D., Liu, K.B., & Shi, X.Y.: Communication cable factory at town J, a case study in *The investigations of China's township and village enterprises in*

1990s, R. Ma, J. Wong, H.S. Wong, & M. Yang, ed., Oxford University Press. 1994. (in Chinese)

Walder, A.G.: Organized dependency and cultures of authority in Chinese industry, *Journal of Asian Studies*, XLIII (1983): 51-76.

Wright, P.M., & McMahan, G.C.: Theoretical perspectives for strategic human resource management, *Journal of Management*, 18 (1992): 295-320.

Zeng, D.X.: On the attraction of foreign direct investment and introduction of technology, in P.K. Lau, ed.: *The Trend of China's Economy in 1994*. Commercial Books Limited Co., Hong Kong. 1994. pp. 126-131.

Zhu, C.J. & Dowling, P.J.: The important of the economic system upon human resource management practices in China, *Human Resource Planning*, 17 (1994): 1-21.

Zucker, L.G.: Institutional theories of organizations, *Annual Review of Sociology*, 13 (1987): 443-464.

Sampling and Selection Bias in International Collaborative Alliance Research: Is It Clouding Our Vision?

Veronica Horton
Brenda Richey

SUMMARY. This paper argues that our understanding of international collaborative alliances is limited by selection bias. Bias in data sets developed both from published announcements of alliance formation and in more narrowly focused studies are discussed. The results of an empirical test of geographic bias are reported. *[Article copies available for a fee from The Haworth Document Delivery Service: 1-800-342-9678. E-mail address: getinfo@haworthpressinc.com <Website: http://www.haworthpressinc.com>]*

INTRODUCTION

Interest in and research on collaborative alliances has exploded in recent years. Numerous researchers [e.g., Hennart 1988; Buckley and Casson 1988; Ring and Van de Ven 1992] have conducted impressive

Veronica Horton is affiliated with the University of Akron.

Brenda Richey is affiliated with Florida Atlantic University.

Address correspondence to: Veronica Horton, Department of Marketing and International Business, University of Akron, Akron, OH 44325-4804 (E-mail: VHORTON@UAKRON.EDU).

[Haworth co-indexing entry note]: "Sampling and Selection Bias in International Collaborative Alliance Research: Is It Clouding Our Vision?" Horton, Veronica, and Brenda Richey. Co-published simultaneously in *Journal of Transnational Management Development* (International Business Press, an imprint of The Haworth Press, Inc.) Vol. 4, No. 3/4, 1999, pp. 67-82; and: *Culture and International Business* (ed: Kip Becker) International Business Press, an imprint of The Haworth Press, Inc., 2000, pp. 67-82. Single or multiple copies of this article are available for a fee from The Haworth Document Delivery Service [1-800-342-9678, 9:00 a.m. - 5:00 p.m. (EST). E-mail address: getinfo@haworthpressinc.com].

conceptual studies examining alliances and there have been a number of insightful case studies [e.g., Hamel, Doz and Prahalad 1989; Parkhe 1991]. Some researchers [e.g., Beamish and Delois 1997; Horton 1992; Morris and Hergert 1987; Ghemewat, Porter and Rawlinson 1986] have conducted broad, empirical studies examining patterns of alliance formation. Yet, there is still an incomplete understanding of many issues related to alliances. One area that has been neglected to some extent relates to the methodology employed in many of these studies. This paper explores some issues related to "alliance research methodology" that could influence the results of studies on collaborative ventures. The paper presents a discussion of how the ways in which we learn shape the outcome. The discussion is undertaken in the context of exploring international collaborative alliances, but the broader issues of sample selection are, of course, applicable to many other topics. The context appears particularly appropriate, however, because of the current focus on the transformation of organizations through the use of inter-firm collaborations. The paper is not meant as a criticism of earlier works; rather, it is an effort to increase awareness of issues that could potentially affect and limit our understanding of collaborative alliances. The paper is divided into two sections: the first section demonstrates how the choice of data sources can influence research findings on collaborative alliances, while the second section explores how bias inherent in single or two nation studies contributes to an incomplete understanding of alliances.

PART 1:
CONCEPTUAL FRAMEWORK:
ON DEVELOPING A NON-BIASED DATABASE

An initial issue of interest to researchers in the field of collaborative alliances was gaining a basic understanding of the sheer dimensions of the explosion in alliance activity. One of the early efforts at database building was undertaken in Ghemewat, Porter and Rawlinson's [1986] study of the relationship between alliance demographic characteristics and alliance form. The researchers used a data set derived from public announcements in the *Wall Street Journal*. Morris and Hergert [1987] provided a demographic analysis of collaborative alliances using announcements published in the *Financial Times,* and the *Economist.* Similarly, Ellram [1990] conducted a study of alliance activity based on announcements in the *Wall Street Journal.* More recently, Horton [1992] developed a data set from the *Wall Street Journal,* the *Financial Times* and the *Japan Economic Journal* to explore questions of alliance formation, demographics and structure, and patterns of alliance failure, and Beamish and Delois [1997] did a benchmark study of collaborative alliances using a data set developed by combining data from the Maastricht Economic Research Institution on Innovation and Technology (MERIT) with data on Japanese alliances and U.S. collaborations. These studies provide a base from which basic demographic and structural issues can be explored. Interestingly, however, though the studies covered similar time frames, the findings frequently contradicted each other. For example, both Morris and Hergert [1987] exploring alliance incidence from 1979 to 1985, and Beamish and Delois [1987] examining alliance formation from 1980-1989, found an upward trend in the number of alliances formed during the time periods under study, while Ghemewat, Porter and Rawlinson found a weak downward trend in the number of alliances formed from 1970 to 1982.

Our first goal in this paper is to demonstrate the potential effect of the choice of research design on research findings and the interpretation of these findings. To that end, we have chosen to focus on a relatively simple issue, that of the magnitude of alliance formation and its geographic distribution. We have chosen to focus on this particular issue because studies that explore the broad demographic trends of alliances [e.g., Ghemewat, Porter and Rawlinson 1986; Beamish and Delois 1997] provide the framework necessary to test theories developed through conceptual work [Hennart 1988; Buckley & Casson 1988] and case studies [Hamel 1991; Parkhe 1991]. Consequently, it is critical to comprehend potential biases that may affect the results of the larger studies.

Many broad studies on alliances use public sources for their research samples; however, in doing so, a potentially damaging form of bias arising from the public sources themselves may be introduced into the research design. We propose that the contradictions among the studies pointed out above may be a result (at least in part) of a bias that arises from the sources themselves. As mentioned previously, the authors of the broad studies obtained their data from different public sources. We propose that if these public sources were consistent in their reporting of business news, that is to say the public sources were unbiased in their reporting of news events, then the broad studies would show similar findings with regard to the number of alliances formed.

Proposition 1: The *Wall Street Journal,* the *Financial Times* and the *Japan Economic Journal* should reveal the same trend (upward or downward) in the number of alliances reported in a given time period.

Similarly, one would expect that in the absence of a reporting bias, public sources would provide news of alliances formed between partners from around the world, that there would not be a preference for reporting on alliances formed between local firms, or for reporting on alliances located locally.

Proposition 2: The *Wall Street Journal,* the *Financial Times* and the *Japan Economic Journal* should report equally on alliances formed between participants from around the world. There should not be a geographic preference for reporting on alliances involving local firms.

Proposition 3: The *Wall Street Journal,* the *Financial Times* and the *Japan Economic Journal* should report equally on alliances located around the world. There should not be a geographic preference for reporting on alliances located locally.

Methodology

The purpose of the first stage of this research is to demonstrate how the choice of a data source may bias research findings. Data for this study was compiled by examining each issue of the *Wall Street Journal,* the *Financial Times* and the *Japan Economic Journal* for announcements of alliances. The three data sources were chosen to represent each area of the triad countries of The United States, Europe and the Pacific Rim, and thus provide a global perspective of bias. Information collected included the number of alliances formed, the participants involved and the location of the alliance. If an announcement of an alliance appeared in more than one publication, it was only included in the data set once.

Collaborative alliances were defined as long-term agreements to mutually share assets for a specific purpose [Horton, 1992]. The definition excludes agreements in which one partner does not share benefits of the agreement, arrangements designed for investment purposes only, and one-time agreements. The data collection process yielded 4,407 alliances formed between 1985 and 1991.

There are several limitations associated with this type of methodology. First, the research studied the flow rather than the stock of alliances, and consequently does not identify the number of alliances in operation during the time period under study. Second, the data collection process involves the implicit assumption that the three publications report most alliance formations; however, it is important to note that the publications may be biased to reporting on large "newsworthy" firms at the expense of smaller, lesser known companies. Third, the research is limited to the information provided in the public announcements of alliance formation.

Research Findings and Conclusions

The analysis of Proposition 1 required the creation of data sets representing the alliance activity collected from each of the three publications. Linear regression was used to analyze the relationship between the number of alliances formed and the year in which they were formed. One tailed F tests revealed the following results respectively: for the *Wall Street Journal*, a strong upward trend in alliance activity with an F value of 18.513 and a p value of .0126; for the *Financial Times*, an upward trend in alliance activity with an F value of 12.919 and a p value of .0229; and for the *Japan Economic Journal*, a strong downward trend in alliance activity with an F value of 3.025 and a p value of .1570 (see Figure 1). An examination of the data from all three sources combined could not establish an increase in alliance activity over the 1985 to 1991 time period (F value of 2.460 and a p value of .1919) (see Figure 2).

What is interesting about these results is that they clearly demonstrate how the choice of a data source can affect research findings. Depending on the data source(s) selected by a researcher, one could conclude that alliance activity was increasing, decreasing or remaining relatively constant during the time period under study. An analysis of Propositions 2 and 3 provided additional support for these findings.

Propositions 2 and 3 were also examined using data sets obtained from each of the three publications. The Pearson chi-square goodness of fit was used to analyze the distribution of alliance activity. In each case, a strong geographic bias for reporting on local events was established. For example, the *Wall Street Journal* data set indicated that most alliances involved U.S. partners and most alliances were located

FIGURE 1. Alliance Incidence by Source and Year

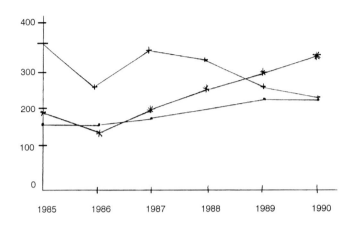

FIGURE 2. Overall Alliance Incidence by Year

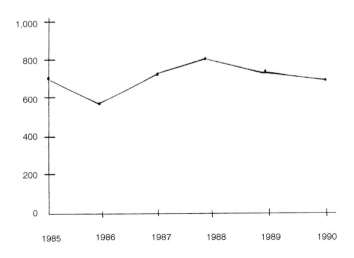

in North America; the *Financial Times* data set suggested that most alliance partners were European and that most alliances were located in Europe; and the *Japan Economic Journal* results revealed that most alliances involved firms from the Pacific Rim and that most alliances were located in the Pacific Rim.

While these results were not totally unanticipated, the extent to which we can be mislead by databases built on a single source or multiple sources from a single geographic region are underscored. For the study of global patterns of alliance activity the use of multi-regional sources must be considered vital. Moreover, these findings suggest that even when multi-regional sources are used, researchers must be aware of potential omissions. While these sources cover each of Ohmae's [1986] triad of world regions, there remains the possibility that international alliance activity in areas of Africa or South America may be substantially under-represented in all analyses of international collaborative alliances.

Other types of reporting bias might also be anticipated, including bias based on alliance form or purpose. Joint ventures involve the formation of a separate legal entity, subject to legal and financial reporting requirements. It appears probable that collaborative activity occurring in this governance mode will more often be the subject of a public announcement than licensing, patent sharing agreements or other less formalized "understandings" between firms. It is also possible that certain industries or products will be more closely covered, particularly "high technology" products, or alliances related to product rather than process developments will be considered more "newsworthy." A researcher employing a data set based on published announcements must remain aware of these concerns.

Should attempts at database development be curtailed because of these concerns? Emphatically not. A study of these databases gives us our best look at the "who, what and why" of international collaborative alliances. It is the development of databases such as these that will provide the empirical base to test the theories developed in conceptual works and case studies. This is already being done in some areas [e.g., Hagedoorn 1993]. Moreover, the alternate response to the lack of data–using a sample of convenience in a more narrowly focused study–carries its own form of selection bias, as discussed below in part two of this paper.

PART 2:
CLOUDED VISION:
THE LIMITATIONS
OF SINGLE OR TWO NATION STUDIES

A second response to the problem of "bad" data is to narrow the focus of the research. For example, Cory [1982] studied all forms of industrial cooperation in Yugoslavia, Osborn and Baughn [1987; 1990] examined U.S. based alliances between Japanese and American firms in a variety of industries, and Ring [1997] explored collaboration across a range of industries using six longitudinal case studies. In a more narrowly focused study, the researcher may be able to obtain access to a pre-existing database. Because of the narrow focus, a "sample of convenience" of this type can frequently avoid some of the problems discussed above. With a more narrow population, the researcher may be able to ascertain that all relevant alliances have been included. Geographical bias in reporting in the *Wall Street Journal* for example, may not present a major obstacle when the subject to be explored is a question involving U.S.-based alliances between Japanese and U.S. firms.

Inherent in these studies, however, is an inability to address broader issues. Of particular concern to international business scholars are the limitations they pose on efforts to study the effects of nation and culture[1] on international collaborative alliance formation, behavior and outcomes. As noted previously, one of the changes that has complicated the study of collaborative alliances has been a growing realization of the necessity of studying these organizational forms in an international context. However, attempts to "internationalize" research have often led to studies that include alliances located outside the U.S. or alliances that include non-U.S. participants, but omit any serious consideration of the effects of national culture on alliance operations. To address the issue of nationality directly, research samples must be designed to capture the issues of interest and any bias implicit in one or two nation samples selected on the basis of convenience must be addressed.

Participant Nationality in International Collaborative Alliances: Is It Important?

Concerns about the lack of multinational data populations reflect a belief that nationality matters in the study of international collaborative alliances. To date, the importance of nationality in international collaborative alliances has not been clearly established. Some research perspectives downplay national and cultural factors. Those who believe in a convergence of corporate behaviors across the globe, feel that internal differences based on a firm's country of origin are merely vestiges of corporate history. Industry and organizational characteristics, not national ones, are the appropriate subject of study. Some studies of international collaborative alliances confirm this belief. Harrigan [1987], in a study of multinational corporations (U.S. and foreign) involved in alliances affecting commerce in the U.S., did not specifically test issues of national origin, but generally found that (organizational) cultural symmetry was more important than national origin in alliance success.

Economic perspectives, such as transaction costs analyses, also tend to discount the role of nationality in favor of more tangible economic issues. When issues of nationality are considered in this perspective, it is the existence of these differences, rather than nature of the differences that becomes the subject of interest. For example, in using transaction costs analyses to explain a multinational corporation's use of joint ventures as an entry mode, Hennart [1988] recognized that a host country firm's knowledge of its national culture is an asset the host firm brings to the alliance. If imperfect markets inhibit the acquisition of this knowledge in other ways (such as acquiring the firm outright), a joint venture or alliance may be formed. This perspective, however, does not encourage questions about the ways in which the national culture may impact venture operations.

Even researchers studying the impact of national and cultural differences in business behavior might question whether attributes that can be determined at an individual level can be translated to an organizational level.[2] For example, could a study indicating that managers from less individualistic cultures work better in groups be used to postulate that firm with national origins in the same culture would be better equipped to function in a collaborative alliance? Although we may not be able to automatically translate individual cultural traits up to the level of organizational behavior, there is evidence that firm nationality counts. Kogut [1991] effectively argued that we do see national differences in "organizing" capabilities and that because these capabilities are so closely tied to the national and cultural settings in which they were developed they are less transferable than other types of technology. It is not a great leap then to suggest that these national differences in "organizing" capabilities affect not only internal firm relationships, but external relationships as well–and that these differences would influence a firm's attitude toward, and behavior within, alliances. Questions that might arise include whether firms from some nations are more inclined to enter inter-firm alliances or are better equipped to operate in those they join. Do firms from some nations prefer or operate more effectively in certain alliance forms? For example, do U.S. multinationals prefer joint ventures over less structured alliance forms because they reflect the highly legalistic nature of the U.S. business culture? They also suggest issues regarding alliances between firms from different nations. Do firms from some nations work better with some alliance partners and less well with others, and what factors determine this?

Case study research on collaborative alliances suggests that national differences exist and impact the formation, operations and outcomes of international strategic alliances [Hamel 1991]. Hamel, for instance, has found in his studies of learning as a key to using alliances as a strategic tool that Japanese firms appear better able than Western firms to learn in an alliance setting. Parkhe [1991] has argued that cultural differences (including ones based on nationality) are divisive, and will eventually lead to alliance failure unless the partners learn to overcome them.

These results suggest that there are a number of national issues that need to be explored to further our understanding of international strategic alliances. For instance, how deep are the what appear to be national/cultural differences at the organizational level? Hamel found that in at least one instance a French partner had become adept at learning within an alliance setting. Do the differences in learning skills he noted reflect a distinctive organizing capability of Japanese firms, or is it possible that Japanese firms started using alliances earlier than other firms or in different settings and so are further along a learning curve? Hamel's [1991] study suggests some of each.

Another set of questions might explore whether Hofstede's cultural dimensions can be used to explain different alliance capabilities. For example, are firms with origins in cultures exhibiting lower levels of uncertainty avoidance better able to deal with the ambiguities inherent in an alliance with multiple partners? Do they choose different governance modes? If not, are there other underlying organizational dimensions that we can uncover through an analysis of apparent national differences [Cheng 1994]?

If Parkhe [1991] is correct in suggesting that cultural differences can divide an alliance, it becomes important to know not just that learning might overcome this effect, but also if the effects are lessened in certain pairings. Can differing cultural attributes be used to evaluate the chances of alliance success? Might some cultures be very different, but complementary? Are there "combinations" that prove more effective?

We lack a clear understanding of how nationality and culture impact international alliances. We cannot develop the necessary understanding if we cannot develop samples that allow us to address the issue. If what we know about international collaborative alliances has been ascertained from studies of alliances between firms from only two or a few nations we have limited our ability to understand the national aspects of international strategic alliances. This also implies that the understandings we have developed based on two nation studies are useful, but may be incomplete. For instance, Osborn and Baughn [1991] studied factors that determine the governance mode in U.S. based alliances between Japanese and U.S. firms. They found that high technological intensity within an industry was associated with the use of contractual arrangements, while the intent to conduct joint R&D was associated with the use of joint ventures. They also noted that size had an effect, postulating that particularly in joint R&D undertakings, a smaller firm joining a larger multinational used a joint venture for protection. Although limiting the study to alliances between firms of two nations provides greater assurance of capturing the relevant population, it limits the questions that might be asked. For instance, would the factors Osborn and Baughn found be the same in alliances that included a broader national range of partners (Japanese-U.K. or U.S.-French)? Would the factors be the same for firms of the same national origin, i.e., would the results have been the same if the study looked at Japanese-Japanese or U.S.-U.S. alliances? Similarly, would Erden [1997] in his study of joint ventures in Turkey have found the same level of satisfaction among foreign investors had he explored alliances located in China?

CONCLUSIONS

Research complexity has increased dramatically with the realization that management must be studied in an international context [Richey and Horton 1995; Boyacigiller and Adler 1991; Adler and Doktor 1986]. If U.S. examples are not typical, or if the U.S. management practices do not reflect the outcome of management system evolution everywhere [Kogut 1991], research formulated on U.S. theoretical foundations and carried out on U.S. populations can provide only a partial picture. As research moves from a national base to a multinational inquiry, however, theory formulation and data collection become more complex, and therefore more difficult to address [Demb 1994].

As inter-firm collaborations have become the "first best choice" for many firms [Hennart 1988], there is an appreciation of the need to better understand these organizational forms.

In 1980, the typical topic of study was a joint venture between a multinational firm (MNC) and a local partner providing the MNC market access previously denied by government regulation or cultural distance [Franko 1971; 1989; Killing 1982]. Relationships were viewed as being permanent, with dissolution or absorption by a single parent reported as venture failure [Gomes-Casseres 1987]. Bartlett and Ghoshal [1992] note that typical of more recent alliances is the presence of two firms from industrialized nations focusing on new technology or product development. The relationship today is often transitional and strategic in nature. This perception arguably reflects both an actual change in firm behavior and a growing awareness of alternative patterns existing previously, particularly in non-U.S. settings.

Together, these changes have added dramatic complexity to the definition of research questions and our ability to obtain data. Previously, researchers might feel that they had achieved a solid understanding of collaborative alliances from studying the behavior of U.S. multinational companies in joint ventures. In fact, Harvard University's database on U.S. multinational companies was the source for a number of studies [Franko 1989; Killing 1982]. Today, however, researchers will find that comparable sources of information do not exist when inter-firm collaboration is viewed in an international context and defined as including both equity and non-equity forms. It has been suggested that data regarding collaborative alliances is "fragmentary and incomplete" [Contractor and Lorange 1988]. Furthermore, there is not even agreement as to what constitutes a collaborative alliance [Harrigan 1988; Hagedoorn and Schakenraad 1990; Horton 1992; Richey 1994; Horton and Richey 1997].

This lack of data presents particular problems for scholars moving from theory development to theory testing. Researchers attempting empirical studies have responded in several ways: some narrow the scope of their research by using a sample of alliances form one or two nations for which data is readily accessible [Cory 1982; Osborn and Baughn 1987; 1990]; others attempt to build data sets from published announcements [Morris and Hergert 1987; Horton 1992; Hagedoorn 1993]. Either approach, as discussed above, is open to bias, and consequently mold our understanding of international collaborative alliances.

This paper has addressed two of the sample selection issues that impact what we have learned about international strategic alliances. There are clearly many others. The discussion turns on the belief that nationality of origin affects firms–a belief that firms have not yet entirely become global citizens with global organizational styles. If no differences would result from studying these differing national combinations, we could claim to adequately understand new organizational forms from the comfortable niche of domestic studies. However, if we suspect that nationality and culture do make a difference, even at the organizational level, we must move to the broader international context. One of the greatest difficulties in studying international strategic alliances is to find an appropriate sample, particularly for large scale empirical studies. There is no central listing of international alliances. One method used by researchers is to build a database from reports in the business press. As noted previously, this method provides a basic understanding of what is happening in the global context, as long as an adequate selection of global sources is used. It also produces a multinational population, and thus the context to study to explore some of the national issues outlined above. A second approach is to employ a narrow "convenience" sample involving alliances from a single nation or a few nations. This method severely hampers the generalizability of the research findings. Both approaches carry with them the potential for other types of bias discussed above.

Parkhe [1993] has argued that the state of our knowledge about international alliances is so rudimentary, and theory development so belated, that we should focus on building knowledge through coordinated case studies. While acknowledging the problems he discusses, as well as suggesting a few of our own, this paper does not go so far. (Nor is it likely that researchers will adopt so narrow a limit on their choice of methodologies.) The aim of this discussion is not to "find fault" with either the attempts at database development or the research of authors conducting studies with a narrower focus. The limitations of time and money shape our ability to conduct the types of studies we would prefer. Rather, it is an attempt to draw out attention to the bias inherent in different samples. Despite the limitations raised above, the research has made valuable contributions to our understanding of international strategic alliances. The intent of this paper is to highlight the limitations of this understanding and to argue for the use, where possible, of broader samples that allow us to explore other important issues. Many researchers recognize the possibility of sample bias and warn us that we may not be able to generalize from their studies. The issue may, in fact, be more relevant to ourselves as research consumers. It is easy for the reader, skimming the ever increasing number of journals that cross our desk, to retain only a one-line summary of the study results. In doing so, we must remember that the one-liner represents a snapshot, and that frequently snapshots reveal only part of the event. We must include in our one-line mental summary a careful understanding of the limitations on applying the findings to a larger population.

NOTES

1. The concepts of nation and culture are clearly separable. Nations may include more than one culture; and cultures may extend beyond national borders. However, for business entities, it is often difficult to separate the effects of the two influences. For example is the Japanese corporate governance model attributable to Japanese culture or to the nation's legal and regulatory policies. Because of the difficulty in distinguishing between these effects, the terms will be used interchangeably. It is hoped at this general level of discussion, the lack of precision will not obscure the overall argument.

2. Concern over this point is heightened by increased cross-national merger and acquisition activity. At what point, if ever, does a company take on the "nationality" of its acquirer? Did MGM become more Japanese after being acquired by Sony? The issue of corporate nationality is too complex to be resolved here, but it is clear that these issues will become part of any discussion of national organization traits.

BIBLIOGRAPHY

Adler, N. and Doktor, R. 1986. From The Atlantic To The Pacific Century: Cross-Cultural Management Review. *Journal of Management,* 12 (2): 295-318.

Bartlett, C.A. and Ghoshal, S. 1992. *Transnational Management.* Homewood, IL: Irwin.

Beamish, P. and A. Delois 1997. Incidence and Propensity of Alliance Formation. In Beamish and Killing, eds., *Cooperative Strategies: Asian Pacific Perspectives,* the New Lexington Press, San Francisco, CA, pages 91-114.

Boyacigiller, N.A. and Adler, N.J. 1991. The Parochial Dinosaur: Organizational Science In A Global Context. *Academy of Management Review,* 16 (2): 262-290.

Buckley, P.J. and Casson, M. 1988. A Theory Of Co-Operation In International Business. *Management International Review,* 28 (Special Issue): 19-113.

Contractor, F. and Lorange, P. 1988. Competition vs. Cooperation: A Benefit/Cost Framework For Choosing Between Full-Owned Investments And Cooperative Relationships. *Management International Review,* 28 (Special Issue): 5-19.

Cory, P.S. 1982. Industrial Cooperation, Joint Ventures and the MNE in Yugoslavia. In A. Rugman, ed., *New Theories of the Multinational Enterprise.* New York: St. Martin's Press.

Demb, A. 1994. The Comparative Challenge: Discovering The "Problem Set". Paper presented at the Academy of Management meeting, Dallas, 1994.

Erden, D. 1997. Stability and Satisfaction in Cooperative FDI. In Beamish and Killing, eds., *Cooperative Strategies: European Perspectives,* the New Lexington Press, San Francisco, CA, pages 158-183.

Franko, L.G. 1971. *Joint Venture Survival in Multinational Corporations,* New York: Prager.

Franko, L.G. 1989. Use of Minority and 50-50 Joint Ventures by United States Multinationals During the 1970s: The Interaction of Host Country Policies and Corporate Strategies. *Journal of International Business Studies,* 20 (2): 19-40.

Ghemewat, P., Porter, M. and Rawlinson, R. 1986. Pattern of International Coalition Activity. In M. Porter eds. *Competition in Global Industries,* Boston: Harvard Business School Press.

Gomes-Casseres, B. 1987. Joint Venture Instability: Is It a Problem? *Columbia Journal of World Business,* 22 (Summer): 97-102.

Hagedoorn, J. 1993. Understanding the Rationale of Strategic Technology Partnering: Interorganizational Modes of Cooperation and Sectoral Differences. *Strategic Management Journal,* 14 (5): 371-385.

Hagedoorn, J. and J. Schakenraad 1990. Strategic Partnering and Technological Cooperation. In Dankbaar, Gronewegen and Schenk, eds., *Perspectives in Industrial Organization,* Kluwer, Norwell, MA.

Hamel, G. 1991. Competition for Competence and Inter-Partner Learning Within International Strategic Alliances. *Strategic Management Journal,* 12 (Special Issue): 83-103.

Harrigan, K.R. 1988. Strategic Alliances and Partner Asymmetries. *Management International Review,* 28 (Special Issue): 53-71.

Hennart, J.F. 1988. A Transaction Costs Theory of Equity Joint Ventures. *Strategic Management Journal,* 9 (4): 361-374.

Hofstede, G. 1980. *Culture's Consequences: International Differences in Work-Related Values.* Beverly Hills: Sage Publications.

Horton, V. 1992. *Strategic Alliances: An Exploration of Their Incidence, Configuration and Transformation in Europe, North America and the Pacific Rim from 1985 to 1991,* PhD dissertation Ohio State University: Columbus, OH.

Horton, V. and B. Richey 1997. On Developing a Contingency Model of Technology Alliance Formation. In Beamish and Killing, eds., *Cooperative Strategies: North American Perspectives*, the New Lexington Press, San Francisco, CA, pages 89-110.

Killing, J.P. 1982. How to Make a Global Joint Venture Work. *Harvard Business Review*, 60 (3): 120-127.

Kogut, B. 1988. A Study of the Life Cycle of Joint Ventures. *Management International Review*, 28 (Special Issue): 39-52.

Kogut, B. 1991. Country Capabilities and the Permeability of Borders. *Strategic Management Journal*, 12 (Special Issue): 33-47.

Morris, D. and Hergert, M. 1987. Trends in International Collaborative Agreements. *Columbia Journal of World Business*, 22 (Summer): 15-21.

Ohmae, K. 1986. Becoming a Triad Power: The New Global Corporation. *International Marketing Review*, August: 7-20.

Osborn, R.N. & Baughn, C.C. 1990. Forms of Interorganizational Governance for Multinational Alliances. *Academy of Management Journal*, 33 (3): 503-519.

Parkhe, A. 1991. Interfirm Diversity, Organizational Learning and Longevity in Global Strategic Alliances. *Journal of International Business Studies*, 22 (4): 579-601.

Parkhe, A. 1993. 'Messy' Research, Methodological Predispositions and Theory Development in International Joint Ventures. *Academy of Management Review*, 18: 227-268.

Richey, B.E. 1994. *EUREKA's First Years: A Study of Alliances Formed Under the Auspices of the European Research Cooperation Agency*, PhD dissertation, Ohio State University: Columbus OH.

Richey B. and V. Horton 1995. Feeling Our Way in the Dark: How the Lack of "Good" Data Shapes Our Understanding of International Strategic Alliances. Presented at the 1995 Academy of Management Meeting, Vancouver CA.

Ring, P.S. 1997. Patterns of Process in Cooperative Interorganizational Relationships. In Beamish and Killing, eds., *Cooperative Strategies: North American Perspectives*, the New Lexington Press, San Francisco, CA, pages 286-307.

Ring, P.S. and Van de Ven, A.H. 1992. Structuring Cooperative Relationships Between Organizations. *Strategic Management Journal*, 13: 483-498.

Determinants
of Defender-Prospector
Strategic Preferences:
Examining the Effects
of Personality and Culture

Steve Williams
Sunitha Narendran

SUMMARY. An exploratory study involving 273 Indian managers from India and Singapore measured the effects of demographic (age, sex, education, nationality, and culture), personality (locus of control, achievement need, and ambiguity intolerance), and work-related (organizational level, tenure, and organizational size) factors on managerial preference as measured by the defender-prospector (Miles & Snow, 1978) continuum. Blockwise regression analysis revealed that younger managers, male managers, and managers with high ambiguity tolerance were significantly more likely to prefer prospector strategies. *[Article copies available for a fee from The Haworth Document Delivery Service: 1-800-342-9678. E-mail address: getinfo@haworthpressinc.com <Website: http://www.haworthpressinc.com>]*

Steve Williams is affiliated with the Department of Business Administration, Texas Southern University.

Sunitha Narendran is affiliated with the Department of Organizational Behavior, National University of Singapore.

Address correspondence to: Dr. Steve Williams, Department of Business Administration, Texas Southern University, 3100 Cleburne, Room 324 Houston, TX 77004 (E-mail: busgswwillia@EMAIL.TSU.EDU).

[Haworth co-indexing entry note]: "Determinants of Defender-Prospector Strategic Preferences: Examining the Effects of Personality and Culture." Williams, Steve, and Sunitha Narendran. Co-published simultaneously in *Journal of Transnational Management Development* (International Business Press, an imprint of The Haworth Press, Inc.) Vol. 4, No. 3/4, 1999, pp. 83-105; and: *Culture and International Business* (ed: Kip Becker) International Business Press, an imprint of The Haworth Press, Inc., 2000, pp. 83-105. Single or multiple copies of this article are available for a fee from The Haworth Document Delivery Service [1-800-342-9678, 9:00 a.m. - 5:00 p.m. (EST). E-mail address: getinfo@haworthpressinc.com].

The formulation of strategy and the ultimate decision regarding the strategic direction an organization will take has been posited to include at least three elements: what a company *might* do, what a company *can* do, and what a company *wants* to do (Andrews, 1980). Discovering what a company might do entails the identification of potential opportunities and risks, ascertaining what a company can do involves an assessment of internal resources and capabilities, and determining what a company wants to do requires an understanding of the personal values, aspirations, and ideals of strategic decision makers (Andrews, 1980). While the first two components of strategy formulation have received extensive attention by organizational theorists, the impact of individual characteristics on strategic direction is a more recent focus of strategic research (Begley & Boyd, 1987; Haley & Stumpf, 1989; Hambrick & Mason, 1984; Miller & Droge, 1986). Nahavandi and Malekzadeh (1993: 411) have argued that before we can fully understand the factors which influence strategy-making, "one of the basic questions to answer is: given the constant and dynamic formulation and reformulation of strategy, how does the leaders' style affect the choice of strategy?" The present study was developed to test the extent to which managerial differences, especially those associated with personality and national culture, influence strategic choice.

DETERMINANTS OF STRATEGIC CHOICE

A number of theorists have offered dimensions along which managers are hypothesized to vary in their strategy-making (Gupta, 1984; Khandwalla, 1976; Leontiades, 1982); however, relatively few studies have specifically examined managerial determinants of strategy formulation. Managerial characteristics which have been found to be related to strategic choice include demographic and work-related differences (Alutto & Hrebiniak, 1975; Child, 1974; Hart & Mellons, 1970; Hambrick & Mason, 1984; Miller, Kets De Vries, & Toulouse, 1982; Pfeffer, 1983; Song, 1982) and a handful of stable dispositions (Anderson, Hellriegel, & Slocum, 1977; Brockhaus, 1975; Guth & Tagiuri, 1965; Kets De Vries & Miller, 1986; Kimberly, 1979; Miller, 1987; Miller et al., 1982; Nutt, 1986; Saunders & Stanton, 1976). It should be noted that while these latter studies do show managerial differences can be related to strategic preferences, reported effects are not always strong or consistent (Nahavandi & Malekzadeh, 1993; Sexton & Bowman, 1983).

Although psychological factors have been recognized as determinants of strategic behavior by a number of theorists (Barnes, 1984; Bateman & Zeithaml, 1989; Schwenk, 1984), one intrapsychic element which has received little attention is the effect of national culture on strategic decision making (Franke, Hofstede, & Bond, 1991; Schneider, 1989; Schneider & De Meyer, 1991). Since national culture provides the context from which assumptions regarding relationships with the environment and people are derived (Schein, 1985), the social norms and values held by managers have been predicted to influence how strategic decisions are made (Schneider, 1989). That is, the information used by managers to develop strategy is filtered by cultural beliefs such that "the strategy formulation process cannot be considered 'culture-free'" (Schneider, 1989: 149). For example, Kagono, Nonaka, Sakakibara, and Okumura (1985) reported cultural differences among American, Japanese, and European strategy formulation approaches, with American and European managers preferring control-oriented options while Japanese managers preferred more adaptive and evolutionary options. Additionally, Schneider and De Meyer (1991) found that culture influenced strategic preferences, with Latin European managers more likely to prefer proactive and change-oriented strategic choices, and Rieger and Wong-Rieger (1984) reported that strategy formulation in the airline industry appeared to be influenced by national culture.

These findings are indicative of the role culture may play in strategy-making since strategy formulation, which has been recognized as the underlying foundation of the strategic management process creating the context of subsequent strategic actions (Lyles & Mitroff, 1980), has been shown to be derived from the assumptions managers share (Schein, 1985; Van Maanen & Barley, 1983). Culture, which is "the collective programming of the mind which distinguishcs one human group from another" (Hofstede, 1980: 48), provides much of the context and many of the shared assumptions managers use to interpret information and develop strategic plans. It seems likely that the formulation of strategy "will be affected by cultural assumptions [held by managers] regarding the relationship with the environment and the nature of relationships among people" (Schneider, 1989: 162).

STRATEGIC ORIENTATIONS

Miles and Snow (1978) have suggested three viable strategic orientations: defenders focus on establishing a safe and stable niche; prospectors strive for new product and market opportunities; and analyzers combine aspects of both defenders and prospectors. According to Miles and Snow (1978), defenders generally prefer to seal off a portion of the total available market and aggressively maintain this domain through a single-minded and cautious approach aimed at maintaining the status quo. Prospectors, on the other hand, pursue and attempt to exploit potential opportunities and strive to expand their broadly-defined domain through a flexible and change-oriented approach. Analyzers combine elements of the other strategic orientations by simultaneously maintaining established customers and products while locating and exploiting possible opportunities with the aim of minimizing risk while maximizing profit.

Although some have questioned the applicability of Miles and Snow's typology (Hambrick, 1983), research has generally found support for these strategic orientations (Chaganti & Sambharya, 1987; Miles, Snow, Meyer, & Coleman, 1978; Snow & Hrebiniak, 1980; Smith, Guthrie, & Chen, 1989; Zahra & Pearce, 1990). Additionally, this typology has been recommended for cross-cultural strategic research since it "may be useful in differentiating the strategic response tendencies of organizations in different cultures" (Schneider, 1989: 164). However, Zahra and Guthrie (1990) have noted that research using the Miles-Snow typology has frequently suffered from inadequate and ambiguous operationalization problems with a lack of attention to validity and reliability concerns, although these authors do recommend its continued refinement and use. Doty and Glick (1994), who also support the use of this strategic characterization system, have pointed out that while the Miles-Snow typology is rich in "feeling," it does not provide the unambiguous definitions that are necessary for rigorous testing, forcing researchers to develop and refine their own means of examining theoretical relationships. Mindful of these limitations, the Miles and Snow strategic orientations of defender, prospector, and analyzer were used to measure managerial strategic preference in this study.

Meyer (1982) has argued that managers with a prospector orientation are more likely to be proactive and entrepreneurial in their strategic choices than managers with defender orientations, and Miles et al.

(1978) report that managers pursuing a defender orientation tend to be more traditional and conservative in their beliefs, as opposed to prospectors who tend to be flexible and responsive; analyzers exhibit characteristics in common with both defenders and prospectors. A similar strategic distinction has been made by Nahavandi and Malek-zadeh (1993) who suggest that managers differ in their preferences for seeking challenge, desire of potential risk, and degree of future-orientation, with some preferring challenging high risk strategies while others prefer to "avoid risk and focus on maintenance of the status quo by formulating strategies that require only minimal adjustments in the organization's functioning" (p. 414). Strategies like the former which entail challenge, change, and innovation are typified by Miles and Snow's prospector orientation, while strategies of low risk and maintenance of well-defined domains are characterized by a defender orientation. One means of conceptualizing this typology is as a continuum (Doty & Glick, 1994; Zahra & Pearce, 1990) along which strategic preference varies, with conservative and cautious defenders anchoring one end, change-oriented and aggressive prospectors anchoring the opposite pole, and analyzers falling somewhere near the midpoint. In other words, managers who prefer a defender strategic preference are posited to be more traditional and risk averse than managers who prefer more entrepreneurial and proactive prospector strategies, while those with an analyzer strategic preference are believed to combine elements of both extremes.

HYPOTHESES

An exploratory study was undertaken to test the effects of managerial characteristics on strategic preferences, with a specific focus on managerial personality and national culture. Work by Hambrick and Mason (1984) and others has shown that a number of demographic and work-related characteristics like age, background, education, and so on, can affect strategic choice, and a handful of studies have suggested stable individual differences can influence the strategic formulation process. Although relatively few strategic analyses have incorporated managerial personality traits as predictors of strategic behavior, related organizational research has established that managerial dispositions can influence important organizational outcomes (Tett, Jackson, & Rothstein, 1991). The predicted determinants of strategic choice used in this study were gathered from a review of the strategic literature, which suggested a number of probable candidates (see Figure 1). While the hypotheses are stated in terms of the polar ends of the defender and prospector continuum outlined above, it was also assumed that analyzer strategic preferences, as a midrange or combination approach, would fall somewhere between these two extremes.

FIGURE 1. Determinants of Managerial Strategic Preference

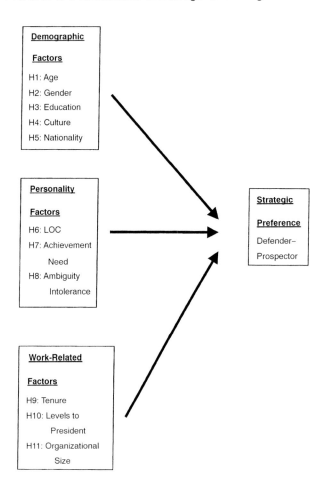

Demographic Differences and Strategic Preferences

Age. An individual's age has been shown to influence strategic preference, with younger managers tending to prefer riskier and more innovative strategic choices (Alutto & Hrebiniak, 1975; Child, 1974; Hart & Mellons, 1970; Pfeffer, 1983; Smith et al., 1989). Wiersema and Bantel (1992) have suggested that flexibility decreases and rigidity and resistance to change increase as managers age due to potential concerns over managerial financial and career security. Therefore, it was predicted that older managers would be more conservative in their strategic preferences, preferring defender strategies, while younger managers would be more aggressive, preferring prospector strategies.

> Hypothesis 1: Managerial preference for defender strategies will increase as age increases.

Gender. Gender-related research has shown how few women advance to higher management levels (Ohlott, Ruderman, & McCauley, 1994), which makes it difficult to test whether gender differences may exist between male and female managers' strategy formulation, especially at senior management levels. An exploratory element of the current project was to examine if sex-related strategic preference differences existed between female and male managers, with the prediction that male managers would be more likely to prefer prospector strategies while female managers would prefer defender strategies. Tentative support for this hypothesis comes from the risk literature which has found that females are generally more risk averse than males (Bromiley & Curley, 1992), suggesting that women might be more cautious and conservative in their strategic approaches.

> Hypothesis 2: Male managers will have a greater preference for prospector strategies than female managers.

Education. Becker (1970) reported that higher levels of education led to heightened innovation, while MacCrimmon and Wehrung's (1986) risk study found that risk-seeking behavior was positively related to educational level. Similarly, Wiersema and Bantel (1992) reported that firms run by managers with higher levels of education were more likely to seek strategic change. It may be that increased education leads to increased awareness and receptivity to the need for and desirability of change. Therefore:

Hypothesis 3: Managers with higher levels of education will prefer prospector strategies.

Culture. National culture is predicted to influence strategy formulation since the assumptions underlying how information is acquired and interpreted by managers are "embedded in social norms and acquire symbolic value as a function of a particular set of beliefs in a particular set of cultures" (Schneider, 1989: 149). Environmental assessment and other organizational concerns derived by managers, such as perceptions of environmental uncertainty or the amount of perceived organizational control over extraneous factors, are believed to be affected by national culture (Hofstede, 1980), and national culture has been shown to influence how managers interpret and respond to strategic issues (Schneider & De Meyer, 1991).

Culture has been recognized as an important determinant of organizational values, attitudes, and behaviors (Hofstede, 1980), but the overwhelming majority of comparative management studies assessing cultural differences have suffered from inadequate operational definitions of culture and have incorrectly assumed that culture can be described by national borders (Adler, Doktor, & Redding, 1986; Nasif, Al-Daeaj, Ebrahimi, & Thibodeaux, 1991). Additionally, much cross-cultural research has fallen prey to the "ecological fallacy" of inferring that specific individuals within a country are representative of the society's culture–most cultural scales measure macro-level societal differences which cannot account for variation at the individual level (Dorfman & Howell, 1988).

To address these methodological concerns, the traditionalism-modernity scale (Inkeles, 1977; Nedd, 1989; Nedd & Marsh, 1980) was used in this study to locate individuals along a continuum anchored at one extreme by attachment to the syndrome of traditional values which include respect for authority, an emphasis on conformity, and the maintenance of established societal practices, and anchored at the opposite pole by attachment to modern values such as openness to social mobility, willingness to change, and independence (Nedd & Marsh, 1980). That is, individuals with traditional values are those who resist change and who perceive conformity to past practices as sacred and important, while individuals with more modern cultural values tend to be future-oriented, regarding change as necessary and desirable. This operationalization of culture seems particularly relevant to the understanding of managerial strategic preferences since individuals who embrace "traditional" cultural values would likely prefer strategies which are cautious and which maintain the status quo (i.e., a defender strategic preference) while individuals who espouse "modern" cultural values would likely prefer strategies which are more change-oriented and innovative (i.e., a prospector strategic preference). Following this assumption, it was predicted that:

> Hypothesis 4: Managers with traditional cultural values will prefer defender strategies while managers with modern cultural values will prefer prospector strategies.

Nationality. Culture was hypothesized to have a direct effect on strategic preference as outlined above; however, studies by Schneider and De Meyer (1991), Kagono et al. (1985), and Rieger and Wong-Rieger (1984) have found that managerial strategy formulation differs by nationality. Although it has been argued that national borders do not necessarily define cultural affiliation, an exploratory aspect of this study was to determine if managerial strategic preference was influenced by nationality. In line with the predicted influence of cultural attachment rather than national affiliation on managerial strategic preference, it was predicted that:

> Hypothesis 5: No national differences in strategic preferences will emerge between managers from India and Singapore.

Personality and Strategic Preferences

Locus of Control. One stable individual difference which has received some attention in the strategic literature is locus of control (LOC) or the extent to which individuals believe future events can be influenced by their actions (Rotter, 1966). Govindarajan (1988) reported that managerial LOC can affect SBU performance–internal LOC managers performed better in SBUs when using a differentiation strategy while external LOC managers performed better in SBUs when using cost leadership strategies. Miller and Friesen (1982) reported a relationship between internal beliefs held by executives and strategic innovation, Anderson et al. (1977) found internal preferences to be more adaptive to change, and Brockhaus (1975) found internal LOC to be predictive of entrepreneurial strategic preferences. Finally,

Miller et al. (1982) have shown that CEO locus of control is related to several strategic aspects, such as preference for research and development, frequency of product changes, and emphasis on differentiation. As suggested by this previous research, it was predicted that managers with an internal LOC would exhibit prospector preferences while those with an external LOC would exhibit defender preferences.

> Hypothesis 6: Preference for prospector strategies will be higher for managers with an internal locus of control.

Need for Achievement. Need for achievement has been argued to motivate individuals to seek out challenging situations with moderate levels of riskiness and has been found to be associated with entrepreneurial preferences (McClelland, 1961). Studies involving entrepreneurs have demonstrated that managers with higher achievement needs tend to prefer more aggressive strategic options which can potentially result in higher performance levels (Begley & Boyd, 1987; Sexton & Bowman, 1985). Therefore, it was predicted that managers with higher achievement motivation would prefer prospector strategies while those with lower achievement needs would prefer defender strategies.

> Hypothesis 7: Preference for prospector strategies will be higher for managers with high achievement motivation.

Tolerance for Ambiguity. Tolerance of ambiguity measures the extent to which individuals perceive uncertain and ill-defined situations as threatening (Martin & Westie, 1959), and some theorists have suggested that those with high ambiguity tolerance may actively seek out unstructured and less predictable opportunities (MacDonald, 1970), while others have observed that managers confronted with similar environments can perceive varying amounts of uncertainty (Paine & Anderson, 1977). Budner (1962) argued that intolerance of ambiguity may be affiliated with rigid and stereotypical responses to new situations, and Begley and Boyd (1987) reported that higher ambiguity intolerance in managers was related to an inability to respond to environmental changes. Based on these previous findings, it was predicted that managers with higher levels of ambiguity tolerance would exhibit prospector preferences while ambiguity intolerant managers would exhibit defender preferences.

Hypothesis 8: Preference for prospector strategies will be higher for managers with higher ambiguity tolerance.

Work-Related Differences and Strategic Preferences

Managerial Level. One work-related characteristic which may influence strategic preferences is managerial level. Work by MacCrimmon and Wehrung (1986) has shown that higher-level executives like CEOs prefer riskier options than lower-level managers, which suggests that higher-level managers, as measured by the number of levels between the manager and the company president, are likely to prefer prospector strategies while lower-level managers are more likely to prefer defender strategies. Accordingly:

Hypothesis 9: Preference for prospector strategies will increase as managerial level increases.

Size. Strategic theorists have also suggested that organizational size is often related to bureaucratic procedures and practices (Astley, 1985; Kimberly, 1976) and have reported that the resulting decentralization and power redistribution deriving from increases in organizational size tend to reduce the impact managers have on strategy formulation (Kets De Vries & Miller, 1986). Similarly, Smith, Guthrie, and Chen (1989) have shown that organizational size moderates the link between strategic preferences and performance. These findings suggest that pressures related to company size may restrict strategic preference such that managers in larger organizations will be more likely to prefer defender strategies while managers in smaller companies will be more likely to prefer prospector strategies.

Hypothesis 10: Managers in smaller firms will prefer prospector strategies.

Tenure. Managerial experience as measured by job tenure has been suggested as a determinant of executive strategic preferences, although existing evidence is equivocal (Zahra & Pearce, 1990). For example, Hambrick and Mason (1984) reported that managers with less experience tend to be more innovative in their strategic preferences while others (Reed & Reed, 1987; Smith et al., 1989) have uncovered no relationship between managerial experience level and strategy formulation. Tenure in this study was measured as the number of years managers had occupied their current managerial position. It was anticipated that managers with lower levels of experience as measured by fewer years in their present position would prefer a prospector strategy, while managers with more years in each would prefer defender strategies. That is:

Hypothesis 11: Preference for defender strategies will increase as managerial tenure increases.

Figure 1 summarizes the relationships predicted in the hypotheses outlined above.

METHOD

Sample. Participants in this study, which was part of a larger comparative management project, were 273 ethnic Indian managers from India and Singapore (where Indians comprise approximately 8% of the total population). In an attempt to increase generalizability, managers in industries such as manufacturing, banking, transportation, information technology, trading, consulting, and others were contacted in the major Indian metropolitan areas of Bangalore, Bombay, Calcutta, Delhi, and Madras, as well as in the city-state of Singapore. Initial contact within the various organizations was typically made through a single manager, usually with the human resource or personnel department, who was asked to distribute copies of the survey instrument to managerial staff who expressed a willingness to participate; follow-up calls were made to those companies who agreed to take part in the survey to expedite response return. A total of 188 Indian and 85 Singaporean managers from over one hundred organizations returned completed questionnaires. All subjects were fluent in English, the language used for the survey instrument.

Respondents' average age was 38, 85% were male, 79% had a university degree or above, 85% were from middle or senior management positions, the average length of employment in their present position was 4 years, and 54% worked in organizations which employed over 1,000 employees.

Strategic Preference. Strategic preference was measured using three business scenarios derived from Miles and Snow's (1978) typology.

These situations were selected from a larger pool of possible scenarios which were pilot tested using almost 200 managers.

Respondents were presented with three short summaries reflecting varying business conditions and asked to indicate the extent to which they agreed with a subsequent prospector strategic option anchored with 1 = not at all and 5 = completely. The first scenario addressed strategic preference under relatively stable conditions by stating: "Your company, though seen as a solid member of its industry with large financial reserves, is slowly falling behind with respect to market share and profitability. As CEO, to what extent would you" followed by "introduce policies that encourage flexibility and responsiveness to the changing environment" (e.g., enter new markets, etc.).

The second scenario offered a positive situation: "You are the CEO of a highly successful company with large cash reserves. Due to a slump in the economy, a number of businesses which are experiencing severe difficulties are up for sale at very low prices. To what extent would you . . . " The prospector option which followed asked: "use the opportunity and take over businesses unrelated to your current business, but which seem attractive in terms of prices and prospects."

The final scenario involved a decision related to the degree of acceptable risk under somewhat negative conditions where the manager's company has had minor financial difficulties and is trying to improve its competitive position. As the chairman of the budgetary committee, the manager was asked to what extent would he or she recommend a project which is viewed as risky due to a high possibility of failure but which would, if successful, yield a much higher rate of return than the 8% the company is currently making.

Confirmatory factor analysis using the three prospector items resulted in a single factor for the three responses, with loadings for the first item of .72, for the second item of .81, and for the third item of .76, supporting that the prospector items were a unidimensional construct. Therefore, the three items were summed (PROSPECT), resulting in a strategic preference scale (mean = 8.7, S.D. = 3.7) where higher values indicate prospector orientations and lower values represent defender preferences; this scale exhibited a reliability coefficient of .64. Although the Cronbach's alpha was marginally low (Nunnally, 1978), it should be noted that weak reliability is only cause for concern if the null hypothesis is rejected (Cook & Campbell, 1979).

Personality Measures. Managerial locus of control (LOC) was measured using eight items derived from Rotter's (1971) LOC scale which exhibited a coefficient alpha of .65. This scale uses dichotomous choices, coded as 1 and 2, which typify either internal or external control orientations. Answers were recoded so higher scores indicated an internal locus of control, and the sample mean was 13.8 (S.D. = 1.7).

Need for achievement (ACHIEVE) was measured using the 20-item Jackson (1966) achievement motivation scale which utilizes a true-false format; achievement scores were coded as 2 and non-achievement scores were coded as 1. For this study, the reliability coefficient was .78 and the sample mean was 34.5 (S.D. = 3.6), with higher scores indicating higher levels of need for achievement.

Intolerance of ambiguity (AMBI) was measured using an eight-item instrument developed by Martin and Westie (1959). This 5-point interval scale had a sample mean of 21.7 (S.D. = 6.5) with a Cronbach's alpha of .85; lower scores indicated higher levels of tolerance of ambiguity.

Assessing Culture. Culture was measured using a condensed version of the traditionalism-modernity scale developed by Nedd and Marsh (1979; Nedd, 1992). This 21-item instrument calculates value dimensions which have been demonstrated to be relevant in placing individuals along the traditional-modern continuum. Respondents were asked to select one of two contrasting statements and then to indicate the strength of their preference for the chosen alternative using a 5-point interval scale. Selection of one option was indicative of traditional values while selection of the opposing alternative demonstrated attachment to modern values. For analysis purposes, items were converted into a 10-point scales, with lower responses indicating traditional values and higher numbers indicating modern values.

The 21 items were summed (TRADMOD) resulting in a traditionalism-modernity continuum, with lower scores indicative of traditionalism and higher scores indicative of modernity. For this sample, the mean was 149.7 (S.D. = 18.5) and the coefficient alpha of reliability was .66.

ANALYSIS

Table 1 presents the correlation matrix for the variables used in this study. AGE was a continuous variable; SEX was coded as 1 = male

TABLE 1. Correlation Matrix

Variable	1	2	3	4	5	6	7	8	9	10	11
1. Age	–										
2. Sex	– .20	–									
3. Educ	– .01	– .02	–								
4. Tradmod	.05	– .07	– .01	–							
5. Nation	– .11	.18	– .05	– .04	–						
6. LOC	.01	– .25	.06	.14	– .04	–					
7. Achieve	.02	– .19	.10	.20	– .11	.38	–				
8. Ambi	.10	– .11	– .09	.00	– .28	.00	.09	–			
9. Level	.22	– .08	.01	.04	.19	.13	.15	– .04	–		
10. Tenure	.42	– .05	– .11	.00	.08	– .05	– .07	.16	.15	–	
11. Size	.04	.03	– .05	.07	– .10	.06	– .29	– .02	– .29	– .06	–
12. Prospect	– .23	.02	.02	.07	.08	.11	.13	– .15	.08	– .18	.02

$(.10 < .05), (.14 < .01), (.19 < .001)$

and 2 = female; education (EDU) was coded 1 = high school completed, 2 = college graduate, 3 = post-graduate; nationality (NATION) was coded as 1 = India and 2 = Singapore; levels to CEO (LEVEL) was coded 1 = five or more levels, 2 = four levels, 3 = three levels, 4 = two levels, 5 = one level, and 6 = CEO; and organizational size (SIZE) was coded 1 = less than 1,000, 2 = 1,001-2,000, 3 = 2,001-3,000, 4 = 3,001-4,000, 5 = 4,001-5,000, and 6 = 5,000+.

Inspection of the correlation matrix reveals support for hypothesis 1, with younger managers significantly more likely to express stronger prospector preferences than older managers. Similarly, managers with an internal LOC, managers with higher achievement needs, and managers with lower ambiguity intolerance were also more likely to prefer prospector strategies, as predicted in hypotheses 6, 7, and 8. Finally, the hypothesis that preference for prospector strategies would increase as managerial level increased (hypothesis 9) was supported with a significant ($p < .01$) correlation of – .18 with prospector preferences (recollect that managerial level was coded such that lower numbers indicated higher levels). While some of the remaining correlations approached significance (e.g., sex, culture, nation, and level), the balance of the hypotheses were not supported.

Since many of the independent variables demonstrated high multi-collinearity with one another, a blockwise multiple regression analysis was performed to control for shared variance and to test the extent to which the independent variables influenced strategic preferences (Pedhazur, 1982). To control for experiment-wise alpha inflation, the variance explained by a block of variables is required to be significant before individual variable contribution can be assessed, following the logic of the Fisher protected (LSD) test. The independent variables were classified into a demographic block of age, sex, education, culture, and nationality for Step 1; a personality block of locus of control, ambiguity intolerance, and achievement need for Step 2; and a work-related block of organizational size, tenure, and levels to president for the final step. The blockwise change in R^2, standardized regression coefficients (i.e., beta, which is recommended (Pedhazur, 1982) for use when comparing the effects of different variables within a single sample), and F significance of all variables entered in the regression equation are displayed in Table 2.

Age (beta $= -.25$; $p < .000$) and sex ($-.14$; $p < .02$) were found to be significant predictors in Step 1, explaining 8% ($p < .001$) of managerial strategic preference. The personality variables entered in Step 2 resulted in a significant (.04) 3% increase in R^2, with ambiguity toler-

TABLE 2. Multiple Regression Analyses

Dependent Variable–Prospector Orientation

Variables entered into the equation	R^2 Change (F Sig)	Beta	F Sig
Step 1: Demographic			
Age		−.25	.000
Sex		−.15	.02
Education		.02	n.s.
Nationality		.08	n.s.
Culture	8% (.000)	.07	n.s.
Step 2: Personality			
Locus of Control		.04	n.s.
Achievement Need		.11	.10
Ambiguity Intolerance	3% (.04)	−.14	.03
Step 3: Work-Related			
Managerial Level		.12	n.s.
Tenure		−.08	n.s.
Organizational Size	2% (n.s.)	.06	n.s.

ance (beta = $-.14$; $p < .03$) the only significant predictor of strategic preference, although need for achievement (beta = $.11$; $p < .10$) approached significance. None of the work-related variables entered in Step 3 resulted in a significant change in R^2.

DISCUSSION

Regression analysis revealed that, as predicted, younger managers were significantly more likely to prefer prospector strategies than older managers. A common assumption held by many is that older managers tend to be more conservative and cautious, possibly being "programmed" by inertia and preferring "tried-and-true" options to new and different ways of doing things. To the extent that this stereotype is correct, it suggests that organizations need to be aware of the possibility that age may influence strategic formulation and choice such that older managers may be more likely to prefer more passive and predictable defender orientations while younger managers may prefer more flexible and nonroutine prospector options.

The hypothesis that male managers would prefer prospector strategies to a greater extent than female managers was also supported. Prospector strategies are considered more innovative than either defender or analyzer strategies (Miles & Snow, 1978), and it may be that men are more likely to prefer innovative approaches than women. For example, Hisrich and Brush (1984) reported that the majority of the 468 female entrepreneurs in their study preferred using established strategies, rather than innovative or modified approaches, although others have found no significant differences between male and female entrepreneurs (Kalleberg & Leicht, 1991). Another potential explanation behind this finding is that women may be socially molded by their cultures to be more conforming and less innovative than men, a possibility which is further supported by related research (Papalia & Olds, 1981; Nedd, 1989).

This study also found that managerial tolerance of ambiguity was a significant predictor of subsequent strategic preference. Managers who were more tolerant of ambiguity and who felt more comfortable with uncertainty were significantly more likely to prefer prospector strategies than managers with lower levels of ambiguity tolerance. Given that a prospector orientation which involves flexibility and a willingness to change differs substantially from a defender orientation which stresses maintaining the status quo and focusing on stability, this finding should not be too surprising. Managers who are comfortable with ambiguity are significantly more likely to prefer prospector strategies which involve heightened amounts of uncertainty and vagueness as compared to more traditional and explicit defender approaches.

As hypothesized, no national differences were found in strategic preferences between managers from India and Singapore; managers from both countries were equally likely to prefer prospector or defender strategies. However, the anticipated influence of culture on strategic orientation failed to materialize since managers with more modern cultural values were not more likely to prefer prospector strategies than managers with traditional cultural values. Similarly, this study failed to find support for the prediction that managerial education influenced subsequent strategic preference. Additionally, neither LOC nor need for achievement were found to be related to strategic orientation, and all the predictions involving organizational factors failed to emerge when tested via blockwise multiple regression. Possible explanations for this lack of support are discussed below.

One possible reason why some of the hypotheses failed to find support may be due to the statistical analyses used. For example, based on correlational evidence, the hypotheses concerning LOC, need for achievement, and managerial tenure would have all been supported. That is, the significant correlations between strategic preference and these independent variables indicate that managers with an internal LOC, managers high in achievement motivation, and managers with less tenure are more likely to prefer prospector strategies. However, when subjected to more rigorous blockwise regression analysis in which partials shared variance (Pedhazur, 1982), these relationships lose their significance. It may be the case that the reported relationships found in previous studies are due to high inter-item correlation; researchers who investigate one or a small number of characteristics can find statistically significant relations which may actually be better attributed to unmeasured variables which share expected or even spurious association.

Additionally, it may be the case that some hypothesized results were not found due to meaningful differences between the sample utilized in this study and previous research. For example, nearly 8 out of ten managers participating in this survey had attained at least a university degree, suggesting a highly educated respondent pool which may have restricted the full range of responses by skewing the sample toward the upper limit of the spectrum. Similarly, the majority of respondents worked in firms which employed 1,000 employees or more, which may have limited the range of useful responses regarding organizational size.

It is also possible that a larger sample size might have been needed to capture the relatively small effect sizes indicated in this study. Some of the anticipated relationships approached significance (e.g., culture, managerial level), suggesting that a larger sample may have been needed to gauge the actual effect size existing in the population. Related to this, other characteristics may be unique to the sample used. Although attempts were made to increase generalizability by selecting managers in a variety of companies and industries, this study relied upon a convenience sample to collect data. The results may have been influenced to the extent that the respondents differed from nonparticipants.

The findings presented here are also limited by the cross-sectional design used to collect data. The results may suffer from same-source bias since all variables rely upon each manager's personal interpretation. Additionally, this study tested managerial strategic preference, which is a measure of behavioral intention rather than actual strategic behavior; existing research has indicated that intentions do not always successfully predict what managers really do (Wicker, 1969). Finally, it may be the case that the low reliability for the dependent variable resulted in attenuated findings. That is, it may be that if a more reliable instrument had been used to measure strategic preference, hypothesized relationships would have been found due to more precise measurement.

Since strategy formulation and the ultimate decision regarding strategic thrust is influenced by the personal values and preferences of strategic decision makers (Andrews, 1980), understanding which and how individual characteristics direct and focus subsequent strategic choice bears further investigation (Hambrick & Mason, 1984). Although many of the characteristics measured in this study proved to be valuable in predicting managerial strategic preference, the large proportion of remaining unexplained variance suggests that a number of additional determinants are likely to exist. Further research may be helpful in uncovering other potentially useful determinants of managerial strategy making.

REFERENCES

Adler, N.J. (1983) Cross-cultural management: Issues to be faced. *International Studies of Management and Organization, 8,* 7-45.

Alutto, J.A. and Hrebiniak, L.G. (1975) Research on commitment to employing organizations: Preliminary findings on a study of managers graduating from engineering and MBA programs. Paper presented at the National Academy of Management, New Orleans.

Anderson, C.R., Hellriegel, D. and Slocum, J.W. (1977) Managerial response to environmentally induced stress. *Academy of Management Journal, 20,* 260-272.

Andrews, K.R. (1980) *The concept of corporate strategy.* New York: Irwin.

Astley, W.G. (1985) Organizational size and bureaucratic structure. *Organization Studies, 6,* 201-228.

Barnes, J.H. (1984) cognitive biases and their impact on strategic planning. *Strategic Management Journal, 5,* 129-137.

Bateman, T.S. and Zeithaml, C.P. (1989) The psychological context of strategic decisions: A model and convergent experimental findings. *Strategic Management Journal, 10,* 59-74.

Begley, T.M. and Boyd, D.P. (1987) Psychological characteristics associated with performance in entrepreneurial firms and smaller businesses. *Journal of Business Venturing, 2,* 79-93.

Begley, T.M. and Boyd, D.P. (1986) Executive and corporate correlates of financial performance in smaller business firms. *Journal of Small Business Management, 24,* 8-15.

Brockhaus, R.H. (1975) Internal-external locus of control scores as predictors of entrepreneurial intentions. *Proceedings of the Academy of Management,* 433-435.

Brockhaus, R.H. and Nord, W.R. (1979) An exploration of factors affecting the entrepreneurial determinants of personal characteristics vs. environmental conditions. *Proceedings of the National Academy of Management,* 364-368.

Bromiley, P. and Curley, S.P. (1992) Individual differences in risk taking. In J.F. Yates (ed.), *Risk-taking behavior.* West Suxxex: Wiley & Sons, pp. 87-132.

Budner, S. (1962) Intolerance of ambiguity as a personality variable. *Journal of Personality, 30,* 201-211.

Chaganti, R. and Sambharya, R. (1987) Strategic orientation and characteristics of upper management. *Strategic Management Journal, 8,* 393-401.

Child, J. (1974) Managerial and organizational factors associated with company performance. *Journal of Business Studies, 11,* 13-27.

Dorfman, P.W. and Howell, J.P. (1988) Dimensions of national culture and effective leadership patterns: Hofstede revisited. *Advances in International Comparative Management, 3,* 127-150.

Doty, D.H. and Glick, W.H. (1994) Typologies as a unique form of theory building: Toward improved understanding and modeling. *Academy of Management Review, 19,* 230-251.

Franke, R.H., Hofstede, G., and Bond, M.H. (1991) Cultural roots of economic performance: A research note. *Strategic Management Journal, 12,* 165-173.

Govindarajan, V. (1988) A contingency approach to strategy implementation at the business-unit level: Integrating administrative mechanisms with strategy. *Academy of Management Journal, 31,* 828-853.

Gupta, A.K. (1984) Contingency linkages between strategy and general manager characteristics: A conceptual examination. *Academy of Management Review, 9,* 399-412.

Gupta, A.K. and Govindarajan, V. (1984) Business unit strategy, managerial characteristics, and business unit effectiveness at strategy. *Academy of Management Journal, 27,* 25-41.

Guth, W.D. and Tagiuri, R. (1965) Personal values and corporate strategy. *Harvard Business Review, 43,* 123-132.

Haley, U.C.V. and Stumpf, S.A. (1989) Cognitive trails in strategic decision making: Linking theories of personality and cognitions. *Journal of Management Studies, 26,* 477-497.

Hambrick, D.C. (1983) some tests of the effectiveness and functional attributes of Miles and Snow's strategic types. *Academy of Management Journal, 26,* 5-26.

Hambrick, D.C. and Mason, P.A. (1984) Upper echelon: The organization as a reflection of its top management. *Academy of Management Review, 9,* 193-206.

Hart, P. and Mellons, J. (1970) Management youth and company growth: A correlation? *Management Decisions, 4,* 50-53.

Hisrich, R.D. and Brush, C. (1984) The woman entrepreneur: Management skills and business problems. *Journal of Small Business Management, 22,* 30-37.

Hofstede, G. (1980) *Culture's consequences: International differences in work-related values.* Beverly Hills, CA: Sage.

Inkeles, A. (1977) Understanding and misunderstanding individual modernity. *Journal of Cross-Cultural Psychology, 8,* 135-176.

Jackson, D.N. (1965) *Personality research form.* Goshen, NY: Research Psychologists Press.

Kagono, T., Nonaka, K., Sakakibara, K., and Okumura, A. (1985) *Strategic vs. evolutionary management: A U.S.-Japan comparison of strategy and organization.* Amsterdam: North Holland.

Kalleberg, A.L. and Leicht, K.T. (1991) Gender and organizational performance: Determinants of small business survival and success. *Academy of Management Journal, 34,* 136-161.

Kets De Vries, M.F.R. and Miller, D. (1986) Personality, culture, and organization. *Academy of Management Review, 11,* 266-279.

Khandwalla, P.N. (1976) Some top management styles, their context, and performance. *Organization and Administrative Sciences, 74,* 21-52.

Kimberly, J.R. (1976) Organizational size and the structuralist perspective: A review, critique, and proposal. *Administrative Science Quarterly, 21,* 571-597.

Kimberly, J.R. (1979) Issues in the creation of organizations. *Academy of Management Journal, 22,* 437-457.

Leontiades, M. (1982) Choosing the right manager to fit the strategy. *Journal of Business Strategy, 3,* 58-69.

Lyles, M.A. and Mitroff, I.I. (1985) The impact of sociopolitical influences on strategic problem formulation. In Lamb, R. and Shrivastava, P. (eds.), *Advances in strategic management, vol. 3.* Greenwich: JAI Press, 69-81.

MacCrimmon, K.R. and Wehrung, D.A. (1986) *Taking risks: The management of uncertainty.* New York: Free Press.

MacDonald, A.P. (1970) Revised scale for ambiguity tolerance: Reliability and validity. *Psychological Reports, 26,* 791-798.

McClelland, D. (1961) *The achieving society.* New York: Van Nostrand.

Martin, J.G. and Westie, F.R. (1959) The intolerant personality. *American Sociological Review, 24,* 521-528.

Meyer, A.D. (1982) Adapting to environmental jolts. *Administrative Science Quarterly, 27,* 515-537.

Miles, R.E. and Snow, C.C. (1978) *Organizational strategy, structure, and process.* New York: McGraw-Hill.

Miles, R.E., Snow, C.C., Meyer, A.D., and Coleman, H.J. (1978) Organizational strategy, structure, and process. *Academy of Management Review, 3,* 546-562.

Miller, D. (1987) The genesis of configuration. *Academy of Management Review, 12,* 688-701.

Miller, D. and Droge, C. (1986) Psychological and traditional determinants of structure. *Administrative Science Quarterly, 31,* 539-560.

Miller, D. and Friesen, P.H. (1982) Structural change and performance: Quantum vs piecemeal-incremental approaches. *Academy of Management Journal, 25,* 867-892.

Miller, D., Kets De Vries, M.F.R., and Toulouse, J.M. (1982) Top executive locus of control and its relationship to strategy-making, structure, and environment. *Academy of Management Journal, 25,* 237-253.

Nahavandi, A. and Malekzadeh, A.R. (1993) Leader style in strategy and organizational performance: An integrative framework. *Journal of Management Studies, 30,* 405-425.

Nasif, E.G., Al-Daeaj, H., Ebrahimi, B., and Thibodeaux, M.S. (1991) Methodological problems in cross-cultural research: An updated review. *Management International Review, 31,* 79-91.

Nedd, A. (1989) Cultural bases of individual differences in compliance-gaining strategies: An exploratory study of Chinese in Singapore. *Research in Personnel and Human Resources Management, 1,* 79-95.

Nedd, A.N.B. and Marsh, N.R. (1979) Social traditionalism and personality: An empirical investigation of the inter-relationships between social values and personality attributes. *International Journal of Psychology, 14,* 73-82.

Nutt, P.C. (1986) Decision style and strategic decision of top executives. *Technological Forecasting and Social Change, 30,* 39-62.

Ohlott, P.J., Ruderman, M.N., and McCauley, C.D. (1994) Gender differences in managers' developmental job experiences. *Academy of Management Journal, 37,* 46-67.

Paine, F.T. and Anderson, C.R (1977) Contingencies affecting strategy formulation and effectiveness: An empirical study. *Journal of Management Studies,* May, 147-158.

Papalia, D.E. and Olds, S.W. (1981) *Human development.* New York: McGraw Hill.

Pedhazur, E.J. (1982) *Multiple regression in behavioral research.* New York: Holt, Rhinehart, & Winston.

Pfeffer, J. (1983) Organizational demography. In Cummings, L.L. and Staw, B.W. (eds.), *Research in Organizational Behavior.* Greenwich, Conn.: JAI Press. 299-357.

Reed, R. and Reed, M. (1987) Internal and acquisitive diversification: CEO experience affects. Paper presented at the annual meeting of the Strategic Management Society.

Rieger, F. and Wong-Rieger, D. (1984) The influence of rational culture on strategy. Paper presented at Academy of Management Meeting, San Diego, CA.

Rotter, J.B. (1966) Generalized expectancies for internal versus external control of reinforcement. *Psychological Monographs, 80,* 1-28.

Rotter, J.B. (1971) External control and internal control. *Psychology Today,* June, p. 42.

Saunders, G.B and Stanton, J.L. (1976) Personality as an influencing factor in decision making. *Organizational Behavior and Human Performance, 15,* 241-257.

Schein, E.H. (1985) *Organizational culture and leadership.* San Francisco: Jossey Bass.

Schneider, S.C. (1989) Strategy formulation: The impact of national culture. *Organization Studies, 10,* 149-168.

Schneider, S.C. and De Meyer, A. (1991) Interpreting and responding to strategic issues: The impact of national culture. *Strategic Management Journal, 12,* 307-320.

Schwenk, C.R. (1984) Cognitive Simplification processes in strategic decision making. *Strategic Management Journal, 5,* 111-128.

Sexton, D.L. and Bowman, N.B. (1983) Comparative entrepreneurship characteristics of supervisors: Preliminary results. In Hornaday, J.A., Timmons, J.A., and Vesper, K.H. (eds.), *Frontiers of Entrepreneurship Research,* Wellesley, MA: Babson Center for Entrepreneurial Studies, 213-232.

Smith, K.G., Guthrie, J.P., and Chen, M.J. (1989) Strategy, size, and performance. *Organizational Studies, 10,* 63-81.

Snow, C.C. & Hrebiniak, L.G. (1980) Strategy, distinctive competence, and organizational performance. *Administrative Science Quarterly, 25,* 317-336.

Song, J.H. (1982) Diversification strategies and the experience of top executives of large firms. *Strategic Management Journal, 3,* 377-380.

Tett, R.P., Jackson, D.N., and Rothstein, M. (1991) Personality measures as predictors of job performance: A meta-analytic review. *Personnel Psychology, 44,* 703-742.

Van Maanen, J. and Barley, S.R. (1983) Cultural organization: Fragments of a theory. Paper presented at the 42nd Academy of Management Meeting, Dallas, TX.

Wicker, A.W. (1969) Attitudes versus actions: The relationship of verbal and overt behavioral responses to attitude objects. *Journal of Social Issues, 25,* 41-78.

Zahra, S.A. and Pearce, J.A. (1990) Research evidence on the Miles-Snow typology. *Journal of Management, 16,* 751-768.

Capacity Building
for Environmental Management
in Indonesia:
Lessons from the Bali Sustainable
Development Project

J. H. Bater
L. Gertler
Haryadi
D. Knight
S. Martopo
B. Mitchell
G. Wall

SUMMARY. There is considerable value in learning from experience in capacity building projects, and this paper provides a self-evaluation

J. H. Bater, a past Dean of the Faculty of Environmental Studies, is Professor of Geography, D. Knight is Administrative Director for Research and International Development, Faculty of Environmental Studies, and B. Mitchell and G. Wall are Professors of Geography, all at the University of Waterloo.

L. Gertler, a previous Director of the School of Urban and Regional Planning, University of Waterloo, is Vice-Chair of the Ontario Environmental Assessment Hearing Board.

Haryadi is current Director, and S. Martopo is past Director, of the Environmental Studies Centre, Gadjah Mada University, Yogyakarta, Indonesia.

All authors were members of the Bali Sustainable Development Project Team which worked together in Bali from 1989 until 1995. This team is now working on a capacity building project in Sulawesi, Indonesia.

[Haworth co-indexing entry note]: "Capacity Building for Environmental Management in Indonesia: Lessons from the Bali Sustainable Development Project." Bater et al. Co-published simultaneously in *Journal of Transnational Management Development* (International Business Press, an imprint of The Haworth Press, Inc.) Vol. 4, No. 3/4, 1999, pp. 107-134; and: *Culture and International Business* (ed: Kip Becker) International Business Press, an imprint of The Haworth Press, Inc., 2000, pp. 107-134. Single or multiple copies of this article are available for a fee from The Haworth Document Delivery Service [1-800-342-9678, 9:00 a.m. - 5:00 p.m. (EST). E-mail address: getinfo@haworthpressinc.com].

regarding the interactive learning approach applied in the Bali Sustainable Development Project (BSDP). The BSDP was part of a larger institutional capacity building and human resource development project supported by the Canadian International Development Agency. Experiences related to contextual and substantive aspects are reviewed. Particular attention is given to the need for incorporating culture into sustainable development strategies, developing an iterative and adaptive approach, and capitalizing on synergistic opportunities. *[Article copies available for a fee from The Haworth Document Delivery Service: 1-800-342-9678. E-mail address: getinfo@haworthpressinc.com <Website: http://www. haworthpressinc. com>]*

KEYWORDS. Capacity building, environmental management, culture, adaptive approach, Indonesia

INTRODUCTION

This paper has several objectives. First, it considers some perspectives related to human and institutional capacity building. Second, it outlines the background to and characteristics of the Bali Sustainable Development Project (BSDP), a specific capacity-building initiative in Indonesia funded by the Canadian International Development Agency (CIDA). Third, it considers some lessons and implications of the BSDP for university-focused capacity building initiatives, with particular attention to cultural, interactive and adaptive aspects, and synergistic effects. Overall, the intent is to share lessons learned in a cross-cultural, development project (Kidd, 1993: 16-25). In that manner, the perspective is comparable to that expressed by Cummings (1993: 143) regarding a project he coordinated in Sulawesi: "There is a need to stop, record, and reflect on the lessons learned from a project." At the same time, it is recognized that tangible indications of capacity building often take considerable time to emerge. In that regard, Grindle and Hilderbrand (1995: 461) have observed that processes for building capacity "are inevitably long, difficult and frustrating . . ., as punctuated with failure as they are with the potential for success." Thus, this exercise in stopping, recording and reflecting occurs at a relatively early stage. Further monitoring will be necessary to learn more from the experiences of the BSDP.

CAPACITY BUILDING

The concept of capacity building has many definitions and interpretations. Indeed, as Cohen (1995: 408) has remarked, "Perhaps no concept . . . is as carelessly used as is 'capacity building'. . . Over the past few years the concept has been diluted by definitional expansion", and in his view this dilution has led to "conceptual chaos." As an example, he noted that in a study conducted by the United Nations Development Program in 1992, a distinction was made among six diverse and inconsistent types of capacity building: (1) macroeconomic policy management (a specific managerial or related skill), (2) professional education (a training task), (3) public-services reform (a structural and legal change), (4) private sector (an untargeted sector-wide focus), (5) popular participation in choice of national goals and means (a political objective), and (6) national development culture (a vague and social system-wide focus).

However, varying interpretations and uses of capacity building are not always undesirable. As Catlett and Schuftan (1994: 168) have observed, "No recipe, standard framework or set of principles can be advocated to ensure the sustainability of institutional change. Each individual circumstance warrants a unique approach." Their comment highlights the importance of being able to custom design capacity building initiatives with regard to the context and needs of the host country, its organizations and its people (Welles, 1995). Nevertheless, it seems reasonable to believe that generic issues exist and deserve consideration in most capacity-building exercises, even if specific actions may vary from case to case. The intent here is to review the experience with the BSDP to determine the way in which that experience reflects such generic issues, to indicate how they were handled, and finally to consider more general implications.

The concept of capacity building here follows ideas suggested by both Grindle and Hilderbrand (1995: 441-463), and by Cohen (1995: 407-422). Cohen (1995: 409) has urged aid agency professionals and academics to return to a well established and narrow definition of capacity building, as expressed in the *Dictionary of Public Administration:* "Capacity building . . . includes among its major objectives the strengthening of the capability of chief administrative officers, department and agency heads, and program managers in general purpose government to plan, implement, manage or evaluate policies, strategies, or programs designed to impact on social conditions in the community." This definition is appropriate, as long as attention also is given to environmental, economic and cultural conditions in communities, and the targets are extended explicitly to include people involved in research and education activities in universities Currey, 1993; Biswas, 1996; Hartvelt, 1996). We also have accepted Grindle and Hilderbrand's (1995: 455) definition of capacity "as the ability to perform appropriate tasks effectively, efficiently and sustainably." This definition requires elaboration regarding what are appropriate tasks, and they suggest that such tasks are defined by "necessity, history or situation in specific contexts." Their viewpoint reinforces the position taken in this paper that "tasks must be specified and assessed for their appropriateness within a given country" (Grindle and Hilderbrand, 1995: 445).

BALI SUSTAINABLE DEVELOPMENT PROJECT

The Bali Sustainable Development Project (BSDP) was one component of an action-oriented five-year development project involving faculty and graduate students at Gadjah Mada University in Java, Udayana University in Bali, and the University of Waterloo in Ontario. Initial consultations regarding the project occurred in both Indonesia and Canada during 1987 and 1988, with the project formally starting in the spring of 1989 and continuing until 1995. It was funded by the Canadian International Development Agency, and was administered by the University Consortium on the Environment (UCE), and the Environmental Management Development in Indonesia (EMDI) project.

UCE had five objectives: (1) institution capacity building to enhance environmental management in Indonesia, (2) human resource development, (3) development of knowledge and methodology, (4) building and strengthening networks, and (5) cooperative activity among the consortium universities. UCE involved two Faculty of Environmental Studies in Canada (Waterloo, York) and three environmental study centres in universities in Java (University of Indonesia, Jakarta; Institute of Technology Bandung; and, Gadjah Mada University, Yogyakarta).

The BSDP was conceived and designed to develop a strategy which would encourage sustainable development, and that could be incorporated into the five-year development plan for Bali covering the period

1994 to 1999 (Van Steenbergen, 1992). The preparation of the sustainable development strategy served as a common focus for various initiatives regarding human and institutional capacity building (such as graduate studies for Indonesians and Canadians, curriculum change at Gadjah Mada University, new collaborative initiatives between programs at Gadjah Mada University and government and nongovernment organizations). As Mattingly (1989: 420) has noted, "Learning-by-doing forces a recognition of the realities of each given situation. It stresses adaptive application of principles and method." The background work for, and preparation of, the Bali Sustainable Development Strategy were intended to contribute to achievement of the five UCE objectives outlined above.

CONTEXT

By the mid-1970s, economic development in Indonesia had begun to gather considerable momentum, a process fuelled literally and figuratively by the newly developed Indonesian petroleum industry. As a member of OPEC, which secured rapid increases in world oil prices as a result of the agreement among producers to control output, Indonesian oil exports earned significant revenues for the government. These revenues made possible a wide range of infrastructure, industrial and social development.

In addition, the Green Revolution helped to spur rice production. By the early 1980s, Indonesia had become self-sufficient in growing of rice. The transformation of agriculture also contributed to the formation of a large-scale domestic chemical fertilizer industry. Industrialization in turn began to change the landscape and, by creating a demand for labor, added another dimension to the rural-urban migration process. Simply put, jobs in industry combined with rural overpopulation to draw even more people to cities which each year grew even faster than the year before. Fortunately, a massive family planning program was an integral part of the Government of Indonesia's development strategy, a program which soon provided tangible results.

Nevertheless, development brought new costs of environmental degradation (Weiskel, 1993; Sloan and Sugandhy, 1994). Chemical fertilizers and constant cropping of new varieties of rice degraded the naturally productive *sawah,* or paddy rice, ecological system. Industrialization brought water and air pollution. Rapid urbanization brought huge numbers of people to cities which were ill-equipped to deal with resulting demands on public health and sanitation systems. In short, economic development, as measured by rising levels of per capita income or net national product, came at a price. Environmental management subsequently was identified as an important but largely missing component in the Indonesian development process.

Indonesian government officials and academics recognized that further education, especially but not exclusively at the university level, was an essential component if environmental awareness were to be raised, if environmental protection policy and legislation were to be formulated, and if environmental programs were to be implemented effectively throughout the country. By the early 1980s, numerous major initiatives to address these needs had been undertaken not only by the Ministry of Education, but also by the then Ministry of State for Population and Environment (KLH), headed for many years by Prof. Dr. Emil Salim who also had served on the Brundtland Commission.

One of the most important initiatives from the university perspective involved the creation by the Ministry of Population and Environment in the early 1980s of environmental study centres at several key universities in Indonesia. These centres were directed to address both practical problems and intellectual issues regarding environmental management and education. The network of centres steadily expanded and was provided with modest financial and material support by KLH. As the rules governing economic development became more stringent in terms of permissible environmental impacts, the university-based environmental study centres were hard pressed to meet the growing demand for professional expertise required to assess and monitor development projects.

There was an obvious and urgent need to increase the number of environmental specialists who could educate other Indonesians. However, within the country only a few universities had the necessary staff or resources to train environmental specialists at the master's and doctoral levels. Indonesian officials recognized that for a sustainable program of human resource and institutional development it would be necessary to enhance the capability of Indonesian universities to train more environmental specialists, especially at the graduate level (Petrich, 1993). With the agreement of CIDA, in 1987 seed money from the Environmental Management and Development in Indonesia (EMDI) project was provided to three Canadian universities in Ontario with well established environmental studies programs (Toronto, Waterloo, York). The seed money was to be used to facilitate the creation of formal "linkages" with three pre-selected Indonesian university environmental study centres. By the end of 1987, three separate linkage agreements had been approved between the University of Indonesia and Toronto; the Institute of Technology, Bandung, and York; and Gadjah Mada University and Waterloo.

The purpose of these linkage agreements was to facilitate arrangements which would lead to long-term commitments on the part of the three "twinned partners" to cooperate in human and institutional capacity building, including staff training. Fostering networking and collaborative work with other Indonesian centres also were prominent objectives. One means of achieving these objectives would be development studies in which there would be collaborative involvement of both Indonesian and Canadian faculty and graduate students. As well, where appropriate, the Canadian experience in developing curricula for graduate programs and courses would be shared with Indonesia. All of these institutions, except for the University of Toronto, formally joined together in 1989 to create the University Consortium on the Environment (UCE), a unique, broad-based CIDA-financed multiyear human and institution capacity-building project with emphasis on environmental management.

In the two years of interaction before the formal creation of UCE, considerable mutual learning occurred. The BSDP evolved from lengthy discussions of possible areas for collaboration between Gadjah Mada and Waterloo. Bali had not been a predetermined choice for the collaborative development study. Various alternatives were explored in depth before the BSDP was selected. In selecting the focus on developing a sustainable development strategy for Bali, the Canadian-Indonesian group was guided by the same conclusion reached by Cummings (1993: 162) that "Projects should build on the strengths of the organizations responsible for carrying them out."

PROJECT ASPECTS

Centrality of Culture

Culture became a core consideration for participants in the BSDP for two reasons. The first reason was common to most international projects, whereas the second was specific to Bali but with implications for other development projects, including those with a sustainable development focus.

The first aspect was the recognition of the significant role of cultural differences as they influence management and operating styles, communication, and collaboration. The second was the unique culture of Bali, and the great importance accorded to culture in Indonesia generally and in Bali specifically. As the Head of the Regional Development Planning Agency in Bali wrote, after the completion of the Bali Sustainable Development Project, he had emphasized to the interdisciplinary team ". . . the importance of Balinese culture as the foundation for development planning in our province" (Rendha, 1995: vi). The result was that culture became a central concern of the sustainable development strategy, a feature uncommon in most sustainable development initiatives which usually focus upon the connections between economic and environmental considerations.

As Kluchhon (1951: 8) has observed, defining the meaning of culture is problematic. Indeed, in his view, "many different definitions of culture are current . . . which may vary in degree of looseness of precision, in the stressing of one conceptual element as opposed to another." The BSDP team adopted the definition provided by UNESCO (1982: 12) that "Culture ought to be considered today the collection of distinctive traits, spiritual and material, intellectual and affective, which characterize a society or cultural group. It comprises, besides arts and letters, modes of life, human rights, value systems, traditions and beliefs." Vickers (1989: 39) echoed the UNESCO interpretation when arguing that "culture is the accumulated habits of many lifetimes, but more than that it is the way people see themselves and organize their lives according to those perceptions."

Most generally, culture was broadly conceived in the BSDP as "way of life," reflecting the aspects identified by UNESCO and Vickers. However, the emphasis is slightly different in the next subsection which considers the incorporation of culture as a central component of a sustainable development strategy.

Culture and Sustainable Development

Although the people of Indonesia represent a diversity of ethnic groups, Bali can be referred to as "a Hindu island in a Moslem sea." Over 90 percent of the residents of Bali are Hindu, while the majority of the Indonesian population is Muslim (Mabbett, 1989; Jensen and Sur-yani, 1992). Furthermore, Balinese Hinduism is vividly expressed in the landscape in literally thousands of temples and through colorful offerings, and is celebrated with elaborate ceremonies, dance, music, arts and crafts (Eiseman, 1989a; 1989b). The landscape and culture of Bali have become a tourist attraction, an official policy of cultural tourism (*pariwisata budaya*) has been adopted, and rapid growth in international tourism has been based in large part on experiencing aspects of the unique Balinese culture. Thus, tourism has become a major force for change in Bali, with considerable implications for Balinese culture and for sustainable development (Wall, 1995a: 57-74).

Sustainable development emerged from the Brundtland Commission as a concept linking economy and environment. However, most sustainable development literature has had remarkably little to say regarding the significance of culture. For Bali, the culture is so strong and its influence is so pervasive that culture was incorporated into the BSDP definition of sustainable development, and the culture itself became an aspect of Bali to be sustained. The translation of this into policy terms, however, proved to be an ongoing challenge.

With a few exceptions, most Indonesian colleagues from Gadjah Mada University in Java were Moslem. Thus, they along with their Canadian colleagues were working in a different culture. In recognition of this situation, at the outset of the project informal links were established with Balinese colleagues at Udayana University in Denpasar, and a decision was taken to conduct a series of village studies at the beginning of the research. The village studies were viewed as an important way of exposing non-Balinese participants to Balinese conditions and culture. Such investigations also were viewed as crucial since the majority of Balinese live in villages, traditional village institutions continue to be very strong, and experience with other development programs such as family planning suggested that such institutions might play an important role in implementing sustainable development initiatives. Further elaboration of the village studies in the context of interdisciplinary development studies of the BSDP is outlined in the next section.

Interactive Approach

Various project components reflected a conscious attempt to design and implement the capacity-building activities in an interactive manner.

These activities included: (1) a collaborative design process; (2) inter-disciplinary development studies, (3) semi-annual and annual work-shops as a mechanism for developing work plans and monitoring progress; and (4) a self evaluation. Each of these is considered below.

Collaborative Design Process

The initial design process had several purposes, including (1) iden-tification of, and agreement about, significant development issues that might be addressed in a collaborative project, (2) consideration of complementary strengths and expertise of people in the two partner institutions, and (3) examination of potential candidate demonstration projects. In beginning in this manner, the BSDP was following the admonition by Catlett and Schuftan (1994: 154) that "frequently, the first step to launch a project is to prepare a series of detailed needs assessments to assist in defining what is wrong and to identify possible solutions." A critical belief from the outset was that whatever issues and problems were to be addressed, they had to be ones which had been identified as important by the Indonesians. The role of the Cana-dians would not be to determine the most important problems or appropriate solutions, but to share their experiences in determining the advantages and disadvantages of alternative solutions. As Catlett and Schuftan (1994: 157) have commented, it is highly desirable for out-siders "to seek advice from those around them who are more knowl-edgeable about the people and the institution they are working for."

While a Waterloo delegation was in Indonesia on an inception mis-sion during 1987, a brief trip was made to Bali because faculty at Gadjah Mada University already had been working there on coastal degradation problems. A meeting was arranged with the Head of Bappeda, or the Regional Planning Development Agency for Bali, who indicated enthusiasm for a collaborative project with the Gadjah Mada-Waterloo team, particularly if it were to examine how concepts of sustainable development could be incorporated into the next Repel-ita or five-year development plan, which would cover the period 1994 to 1999. The fifth Repelita had just been completed, the Brundtland Report had just also been published that month, and yet the Bappeda Head already was looking forward to the next planning period and how Bali would address sustainable development issues.

The approach to the project design can fairly be characterized as collaborative and interactive. It was collaborative in that faculty members from Indonesian and Canadian universities worked together over a two-year period to formulate a proposal which would address issues and opportunities identified and prioritized by Balinese in Indonesia. It also was collaborative in that it involved close consultation with the key government agency with which the project team would have to work to be effective. The design phase was interactive in that over a two-year period various ideas were identified, assessed and modified in the light of new knowledge and understanding gained through discussions and field research.

The design also was interactive in that the phasing of work was modified to respond to the Head of Bappeda's concern that recommendations needed to be completed by not later than the end of 1992 if they were to be useful for preparation of Repelita VI. He was concerned that the rapid pace of change in Bali meant that Bappeda could not afford to wait for a protracted period of time before it received recommendations. Originally, the BSDP team had intended to conduct its investigations from 1989 until 1993 or even 1994. However, to meet the needs of Bappeda, priorities were altered, and work was scheduled so that core activities were completed in time to feed into the formulation of the sustainable development strategy. An important step in the later stages of the project was to share preliminary recommendations with a small group of senior Indonesian colleagues from both government and academia. In this manner, not only were their advice and suggestions obtained before the draft sustainable development strategy was presented for discussion at a workshop in Bali, but it also ensured that they would not be surprised by the contents of the report. After the sustainable development strategy had been submitted to the Government of Bali, the Head of Bappeda stated that the process of preparing the strategy "was truly a collaborative effort", and that the BSDP team had modified its approach to ensure a direct link to the guidelines for development planning in Indonesia (Rendha, 1995: v and vi).

Interdisciplinary Development Studies

Development studies included a wide mix of investigations in eight selected villages, on priority themes (such as waste management, environmental impact assessment, gender), and on selected sectors (such as tourism, agriculture, forestry, small business). In addition, attention was focused on critical areas (such as coastal zones, watersheds, high-altitude steeply sloping areas). The intent was to integrate both "bottom up" (village level) and "top down" (central and provincial level) issues and approaches for a sustainable development strategy. These activities collectively comprised the foundation for a Sustainable Development Strategy for Bali, and were organized into several components (Figure 1).

The concept of sustainable development was interpreted to include not only the continuity of natural resources (basic life supports), but also the continuity of cultural resources (from values and legends, to ceremonies and structures), and not only the continuity of production but the continuity of culture itself (BSDP 1992). Seven criteria (efficiency, ecological integrity, equity, community, cultural integrity, integration/balance, development as realization of potential) were de-

FIGURE 1. Process for Formulating a Sustainable Development Strategy, Bali-BSDP

1 Formulation of Evaluation Criteria	2 Assessment of Conditions and Trends, by Main Themes	3 Formulation of Issues	4 Preliminary SDS	5 Evaluation and Strategy	6 Recommendations
		Flow of Process			
Evaluation Criteria (7)	• Population, Culture and Social Development	Stresses and Capabilities	Strategic Directions • Policies	Evaluation of Preliminary SDS by SD Criteria	Strategic Plan Recommendations to REPELITA VI
Based on:	• Economy: Tourism and Small Industry		• Programs		
SD Concept Bali	• Culture of Bali		• Institutions	Integration: sectoral, spatial	• sectoral
• Ecology	• Environment and Resources		to address issues		• spatial
	• Village Development				
• Development	• Regional Development in context of REPELITA V	Main Issues		Formulation of SDS	• Demonstration Areas–Projects
	• Gender and Development				• Environmental Monitoring System
Workshops	1 and	2	Workshop 3	Workshop 4	
1989	- - - - - -	1990	June/91	June/92	
University-Government-Community					
Communication and Consultation					

rived from the literature and from Balinese experience. Many of the criteria used to judge whether activities were supportive of sustainable development were derived from Balinese customs and concepts, such as *Tri Hita Karana* (harmony and balance among people, Gods and environment) and *Desa Kala Patra* (stability in place and time). An assessment of conditions and trends by main themes, as noted in Figure 1, was then undertaken.

Interest in the grassroots perspective led to research in eight villages to understand the stresses and capabilities at the local level. Such an approach was intended to ensure that the BSDP team would appreciate and understand cultural beliefs, traditions and institutions at the local level, particularly since over 70 percent of Balinese live and work in rural areas. The village field work consisted of participant and field observations, interviews with key informants, and a survey of randomly selected households. A stress-capability framework was used to evaluate village sustainability. Stresses were defined as disruptions in village life and environment, including biophysical, production, human health, cultural and institutional aspects. Capabilities consisted of aspects of these elements that were the bases for overcoming stresses.

Although the interdisciplinary and multi-cultural village study teams were effective, it became evident during field work that the stress-capability framework posed difficulties. The framework and methods, significantly influenced by the Canadians, created problems for some Indonesians who had not had sufficient time to become comfortable with the framework and methods. For example, the terms "stresses" and "capabilities" were interpreted differently by Canadian and Indonesian colleagues, and attempts to apply them in the villages were not always successful.

However, considerable data and insights were gathered from the village studies which helped to provide understanding about general conditions and to facilitate cross-village comparisons (Mitchell, 1994a: 189-211; Gertler, 1995: 389-410; Martopo and Mitchell, 1995: 14-33; Wall, 1996: 123-137). Furthermore, the eight study villages provided a reasonable cross section of the sub-environments in Bali, and of the range of development issues requiring attention. Important lessons from the village work, also encountered in other development initiatives, were that considerable time is required if Western methods are to be used by cross-cultural teams, that misinterpretations can occur when responses are translated, and that local people and foreigners may perceive environmental degradation in quite different manners (Bankoff, 1993).

In addition to the village studies, over 30 position papers were completed by Indonesian and Canadian faculty, staff and graduate students related to themes, sectors and areas. As well, some 20 Indonesian and Canadian graduate students undertook applied thesis research on various aspects of the BSDP. The thesis research provided important conceptual and empirical contributions to the development of the sustainable development strategy, particularly the areas of gender and development, environmental management, and information systems development.

Due to budget limitations, primary data and field surveys were undertaken only for selected themes, sectors and areas. These studies often had to rely on limited information and acknowledged incomplete data from secondary sources. One result was when the draft sustainable development strategy was being developed and reviewed, a few government officials expressed concern about the data being used. They also were concerned that some recommendations were too general to be helpful. However, by the time the final sustainable development strategy was prepared, most government officials agreed that useful information had been assembled and synthesized, and that innovative recommendations had emerged, particularly regarding interdisciplinary and cross-sectoral issues. Further, it was accepted that the BSDP had conducted a clear and useful examination regarding *balance* among the concepts of environment, economy, culture and technology. Project reports emphasized an important marriage between theoretical statements concerning the concept of balance and with Balinese cultural traditions and experiences concerning the concept. Thus, traditional Balinese notions of balance were applied in a contemporary planning context. This approach helped to break the barriers of language and tradition, and brought together researchers from Indonesia and Canada into a mode of mutual learning.

Annual Workshops for Design and Monitoring

Annual workshops were used to report on ideas and findings, to obtain critical evaluation from Balinese and other Indonesian officials, and to allow for *musyawarat* or consensus building among participants. The first annual meeting focused upon identifying development issues, opportunities and constraints. The second meeting concentrated upon methodological issues. During June 1991, at the third annual workshop, a preliminary Sustainable Development Strategy was presented for discussion and review. Following that workshop, the Strategy was revised significantly. The revised version was then circulated to experts in Indonesia and Canada during the winter and spring of 1992, and further modifications were made. What was termed a draft Sustainable Development Strategy was prepared in Bahasa Indonesia and English, and was distributed prior to the fourth annual workshop in late June 1992. At that workshop, 75 participants reviewed the document in plenary and small group sessions. Suggestions from this review were incorporated into the strategy, and it was submitted to the Balinese government in late November 1992. Since that time, the Balinese government has incorporated a number of the recommendations into Repelita VI, or the sixth regional development plan for Bali. In particular, recommendations concerning agriculture, natural area management, tourism, small business, culture, health, waste management, coastal zones, gender, regional development and institutional arrangements were incorporated into the formal planning process in Bali. The Bali Sustainable Development Strategy is available in the Bali Sustainable Development Project (1992), and in a summary form in Gertler (1993: 103-122) and Mitchell (1994b: 145-156; 1995: 537-566). In addition, much of the detailed research which was completed to prepare the strategy is documented in Martopo and Mitchell (1995).

The annual workshops, held in June or July, and the semi-annual workshops each December, allowed the BSDP to monitor progress, and make adjustments in the light of experience. In that regard, the BSDP was practicing Rondinelli's (1993a: vii-viii) advice that

> One of the most promising ways is to use an *adaptive approach* that relies on strategic planning, on administrative procedures that facilitate innovation, responsiveness and experimentation, and on decision-making processes that join learning with action.

In brief, the BSDP put into practice Rondinelli's (1993b: 4) suggestion that the most appropriate approach is one that is strategic, iterative and responsive, or Wiggins (1985: 106) advice that, "In the absence of known solutions, programs have to be experimental." This approach is considered in more detail in a later section focused on the role of adaptive approaches.

Self Evaluation

Before the midpoint of the five-year project, a self evaluation was conducted (UCE 1992). The evaluation involved several components. First, the Canadian and Indonesian program directors developed a set of questions to be circulated to faculty, staff and students involved in UCE. Once the questions had been developed, they were given to all participants (graduate students, staff, faculty) in both Indonesia and Canada. Second, after the respondents had returned their answers, a team meeting was held in which the program coordinators from Canada and Indonesia facilitated a review of the responses, as well as identified actions to sustain positive outcomes and to address problems that had been identified.

Both the Canadians and Indonesians found it very helpful to be alerted to opportunities and problems early in the life of the project when there still was time to take action regarding them. The responses to the evaluation survey were candid, and flagged matters about which other participants had not always been aware. Another benefit of the self evaluation occurred in relation to the end-of-project assessment conducted for CIDA by independent consultants. By the time the consultants began their assessment, due to the self evaluation the project team members already were aware of the major challenges that had required attention, and in almost all cases had been able to resolve or minimize them.

Adaptive Approach

The human and institutional capacity building was based on five objectives specified at the outset of the project. Activities were designed so that deliverable results would be produced relative to the five objectives. At the same time, it was recognized from the beginning that it was desirable to maintain flexibility to learn from experience and to be able to capitalize on opportunities that might arise throughout the project. In that regard, Nelson (1991: 115) has observed that

> . . . it is difficult to envision the selection of a research path which will lead without deviation to an anticipated end-point.

Initial assumptions may come into doubt as the research proceeds or methods prove inappropriate or impractical.

Furthermore, Lee (1993: 9) has recommended use of an *adaptive approach,* one which "embodies a simple imperative: policies are experiments: *learn from them. . . .* In order to live we use the resources of the world, but we do not understand nature well enough to know how to live harmoniously within environmental limits. Adaptive management takes that uncertainty seriously, treating human interventions in natural systems as experimental probes." More specifically, in the context of his work in Sulawesi, Cummings (1993: 163) commented that "the design should be kept flexible enough to deal with changing external situations." Examples of each of these considerations are presented below.

Learning from Experience

The discussions above have highlighted that a basic principle of the BSDP was to monitor and to review experience, in order to incorporate lessons into future activity (Hulme, 1989; Stockman, 1997). This made the annual and semi-annual workshops a core element of the "development study process." The annual workshops were broadly based, and involved internal and external participants from various sectors and levels of government for progress reporting, critical discussion, and Project development as it evolved. The semi-annual workshops involved a smaller number of participants internal to the Project team, and the purpose was Project review and planning at both conceptual and operational levels. At the same time, this adaptive approach created challenges for the project team and for CIDA, with the latter increasingly emphasizing a results-based or performance-oriented mode of operation, and wanting proposals for funding to outline from the outset the expected sustainable results, verifiable indicators and means of measurement, and risk factors.

While the spirit of the CIDA approach is to support the iterative, responsive, adaptive and experimental style urged by Rondinelli (1993a; 1993b), in reality the concern by CIDA for accountability of its funds places considerable pressure on any development project supported by it to provide at the outset specific and detailed outlines of measurable objectives, activities, inputs and outputs–all of which mitigate against the type of approach that proved to be so successful in the BSDP. That is, some of the most effective outcomes from the BSDP were as a result of making changes in response to experience or new conditions, and being opportunistic regarding new situations which emerged in Bali or in other parts of Indonesia as the work progressed. The BSDP experience indicates that the likelihood of a "successful" project improves when there is willingness to permit modifications and changes, even if that means that the kind of "logical framework analysis" that CIDA promotes cannot be laid out with the specificity it would like to see when a proposal for funding is submitted. Fortunately, CIDA desk and field officers, as well as their monitors and evaluators, have been supportive of building in flexibility and adaptation in order for a project to be able to take advantage of emerging opportunities.

Capitalizing on Experience

As noted above, one of the benefits of an adaptive and interactive learning approach was that it helped to create some new opportunities. Some of these are discussed in the following Section entitled "Synergistic Effects." These specific initiatives represented opportunities some of which were identified during the design of the BSDP but then were subsequently modified (tourism, gender), and others which arose after the Project was underway (waste management). However, a common aspect to all of these initiatives was that they provided opportunities to demonstrate how sustainable development action could be taken in specific, well defined situations. In that regard, they are examples of the advice provided by Catlett and Schuftan (1995: 164-165).

> Rather than developing a large-scale integrated development project which tries, all at once, to address a wide range of problems, an incremental approach is preferable. . . . More focused work plans require fewer resources and can mobilize more. Less ambitious project tasks are more easily accomplished, increasing the . . . expectation that the project will succeed. . . . .

Tourism

Tourism is a major force for change in Bali, and became a key element for a sustainable development strategy within which culture was given a central position (Wall 1993: 38-47). Lessons learned from the tourism work in the BSDP also provided a departure point for activity, not identified during conception and design of the Project, in other parts of Indonesia (Timothy and Wall, 1995: 63-73). For example, other funding was obtained for comparative work on the island of Lombok, immediately to the east of Bali (Telfer and Wall, 1996: 635-653). Lombok has not yet had the same intensity of development as has Bali. Consequently, there is opportunity to learn from the experiences in Bali as Lombok considers the role that tourism could and should have in its future development planning. Japanese funding provided an opportunity for one of the team members to conduct ecotourism work in North Sulawesi province, along the coastal area near Manado, which has been targeted by the Indonesian government for substantial tourism-oriented development. With flights now scheduled from Singapore and Manila directly to Manado, that part of north Sulawesi may experience the development pressures that have occurred over the past ten years in Bali. As a result, the work in Bali provided an excellent basis for sharing in Sulawesi (Wall, 1995b).

Gender

The BSDP sought to take into account different gender roles, relationships and needs in Balinese society, and this aspect was woven into many aspects of BSDP activities (Ariani and Kindon, 1995: 507-519; Gupta and Hyma, 1995: 465-487; Cukier et al., 1996: 248-27). During 1992, the BSDP organized and held the first gender and development workshop in Bali (BSDP 1993). This experience, and the partnership with Gadjah Mada University, created opportunities for other gender-related activities which had not been anticipated at the outset of the project. For example, during February 1994, a three-day workshop on "A Gender-Based Approach to Urban Environmental Management Issues in Coastal Areas in Bali" was held. In late March 1995, the Women's Study Centre and the Environmental Research Centre at UGM, in cooperation with faculty from Waterloo, organized a "National Symposium on Gender and Tourism Development" in Yogyakarta, Java (Women's Study Centre et al., 1995). And, during 1994 and 1995, follow up work was initiated through a Sustainable Community Development Project in the Code River basin in Yogyakarta Special Province on Java (Centre for Environmental Studies, 1995). Four major themes were addressed in the Code River project, one of which was gender and development (the others were ecotourism, clean river program (PROKASIH), and community participation) (Women's Study Centre, 1995).

The gender-oriented work helped to create new links between the Women's Study Centre and the Environmental Research Centre at UGM, and among the Women's Study Centre at UGM and various university Women's Study Centres in Balinese universities. In this manner, the collaborative and interactive model served to create new linkages and networks in Indonesia.

Waste Management

BSDP activity focused upon urban solid waste disposal, village waste disposal, and treatment of liquid wastes from garment dyeing operations. Two examples indicate how an interactive approach lead to new opportunities.

One of the opportunities that emerged from the village studies was the need for improved composting and other forms of alternative waste disposal for several communities. A connection subsequently was made with the WISNU Foundation, a Balinese NGO also interested in helping to improve waste management practices. This collaboration led to the design of a new approach for waste disposal and management in the villages, and to the cooperation of community officials. Preliminary discussions also have begun with the World Bank to examine possibilities of expanding a number of waste and water-focused activities in Bali.

For the garment dyeing, much of the dyeing is subcontracted by garment manufacturers to small, family-based businesses which operate in villages. One consequence of the subcontracting is that there often is pollution of waterways from the wastewater which is a by-product of the dyeing process. One of the Canadian team members, working with a faculty member from Udayana University in Bali and with several owners of garment manufacturing businesses, developed a waste treatment process that used locally available technology and materials (Haight and Ratha, 1995: 215-236). Additional financial support for this work was received from the Canadian regional International Development Research Centre office in Singapore.

Synergistic Effects

Creation of a sustainable development strategy requires a multi-sectoral and interdisciplinary approach with attention to the interaction between sectors and the competition among them for the use of scarce resources. For convenience, the BSDP initially divided responsibilities into four major categories: population and culture, environment and resources, tourism and industry, and regional planning. However, these divisions masked more specific interests, such as agriculture and forestry, which required investigation, and broader perspectives, such as coastal zone management, geographical information systems, and gender, which needed to be addressed. Thus, it was necessary to include and involve individuals with a very broad range of expertise.

At the same time, concern with the relationship between top-down and bottom-up approaches to planning, and between the Repelita and local needs, opportunities and constraints, meant that national, provincial and local inputs were required. As a result, a diversity of contacts was made in both university and government circles and, to a lesser extent, in the private sector and with NGOs.

The diversity of contacts and inputs required the assimilation of a large volume and great diversity of information, leading to the generation of new knowledge through the re-evaluation of information in new contexts. It also resulted in requests for individual participants to contribute to other initiatives. Thus, for example, Canadian and Indonesian participants were invited to give guest lectures and to participate in workshops on a variety of topics at project institutions and at other institutions in Bali and elsewhere in Indonesia. Indeed, as the project as a whole and the expertise of individual members became more widely known, invitations were received to contribute to symposia and conferences of international standing. On occasion, funding from such organizations as UNESCO and UNCRD for conference participation facilitated additional visits and project-related work which would have been impossible to fund from the BSDP budget alone. Through involvement in the group project, some individuals identified needs and related research opportunities which could be addressed by themselves and their students, and sought additional financial support. Thus, for example, support for linked initiatives has been received from the Social Sciences and Humanities Research Council of Canada, and the International Development Research Centre of Canada. And, more recently, discussions to explore mutual interests have occurred with the World Bank. At the same time, several substantial programs were initiated through invitation of other agencies which had become aware of the expertise and experiences of project members. For example, in the summer of 1994, an eight-week course in tourism planning and management and a six-week planning course for Indonesian academics and government planning officials were conducted at the University of Waterloo. Such courses increased the wealth of contacts throughout Indonesia for both Indonesians and Canadians, and precipitated invitations to explore opportunities for further long-term activities. Also, several additional initiatives, particularly in ecotourism (Wall, 1995b) and integrated watershed planning (Boehmer et al., 1997), have been undertaken with Indonesian and Japanese government support.

There is a considerable lag time in the initiation of a project, the compilation of findings, the publication of results, the adoption of recommendations, and the evaluation and recognition of the work by national and international audiences. While it is possible to recognize some specific spin-offs from the project, such as an influence on graduate student applications, longer-term implications may be more difficult to tie directly to the project, may be more diffuse, but no less important. Indeed, it is likely that interest in and commitment to development issues in Indonesia and elsewhere will not cease among project participants as a result of the termination of the BSDP. Indeed, activities between Gadjah Mada University and the University of Waterloo continue to be sustained through exchanges under different programs and the development of new proposals, as well as through joint conference presentations and journal articles (Kusumandari and Mitchell, 1997). Furthermore, there is a new group of young Indonesians who have returned to their country after completing overseas graduate degrees, and who now are sharing that experience in their university and government work.

CONCLUSIONS

In this article, we have followed Cummings' (1993: 137-166) advice regarding the need to stop, record and reflect on lessons learned. We have also heeded Cohen's (1995: 419) observation that "There is no agreed 'definition' of capacity building nor could any specialist or aid agency impose one on the field of development. The literature is

too murky and applications too conflicting for this to be otherwise."
Notwithstanding that cautionary note, we hope that the experiences
identified and reviewed in this paper reflect the spirit of the ongoing
self-evaluation which was pursued throughout the BSDP, and help to
identify issues with general value for capacity-building projects. From
the many lessons and experiences, we believe a few are particularly
important.

First, much more attention should be given to *cultural aspects* with
reference to sustainable development. The discussions and debates
focused on sustainable development almost always focus upon the
appropriate balance between encouragement of economic development and protection of environmental integrity. From our review of
the literature, and experience in development work, such discussions
are too often silent regarding the importance of culture, and how it
should be incorporated into sustainable development. Because of the
visibility of culture in Bali, it became obvious that this aspect had to be
a central building block for any strategy for sustainable development.
However, we believe that consideration of culture should always be
given explicit attention in work tied to sustainable development, and
that a focus solely on the balance between economy and environment
is too narrow.

Despite the difficulty in defining culture in operational terms, its
recognition has significant implications for capacity-building projects. Recognizing the importance of culture requires early and systematic consideration of the role of culture in local and informal
situations, as well as in central government and formal institutional
arrangements. It also directs attention to nurturing of practical demonstration activities to illustrate how new ideas can be incorporated
into local practices and not be threatening to well established cultural
values and perspectives. The importance of considering the cultural
dimension is further highlighted by comments from Grindle and
Hilderbrand (1995: 443):

> . . . performance problems diagnosed at the organizational or
> individual level may be so deeply embedded in economic, social,
> and political deficiencies that efforts to improve performance
> must focus primarily on these considerations. Although the im-
> portance of the broader contextual setting for organizational and
> individual activities may seem obvious, a large number of capac-

ity-building initiatives are in fact designed without regard for this environment.

Second, the interactive and adaptive approaches provide opportunities to be innovative and opportunistic over a five-year time period and, in many instances, to respond to opportunities not identified when the Project was being conceived and designed. The BSDP certainly had numerous experiences of this kind, reinforcing the value of arguments by Hulme (1989), Nelson (1991), Rondinelli (1993a; 1993b) and Lee (1993) in support of using an adaptive approach. Learning-by-doing also continues to have great value, as such an approach tends to ground ideas that otherwise might be viewed as unduly theoretical and conceptual, and also forces participants to determine how ideas can be introduced and accepted by people at the local, community level.

However, the BSDP experience also highlights the tensions which exist between the increasing push by funding agencies to be given proposals with very specific objectives, and associated measurable inputs, outputs, and outcomes, and the benefits from allowing for adaptiveness and flexibility. Some of the most innovative outcomes from the BSDP resulted from having room in project budget envelopes to respond to opportunities which could not have been identified, and not likely even have been anticipated, at the time that the project design was crafted. While the need for accountability by funding agencies is understood, it is to hoped that donor development agencies will continue to show willingness to strive for a reasonable balance between results–or performance-based proposals and flexibility to modify objectives and activities in order to take advantage of opportunities, as was done during the BSDP.

Third, the BSDP team devoted considerable effort to develop true partnerships and collaboration in project design, field activities, data analysis, preparation of recommendations, and publications. However, at times the restrictions of limited budget and time combined with too infrequent face-to-face consultations resulted in decisions having to be taken without sufficient dialogue. The potential for misunderstanding and cultivation of lack of trust exists in such situations. The lesson is that careful attention must be devoted to developing genuine working partnerships throughout the project cycle so that the research does not become, or is not perceived to become, unduly extractive by one of the partners (Kiggundu, 1989: 22). The concept of an interactive, partnership approach must be transformed from an ideal to a workable arrangement, which requires sustained commitment on behalf of all partners.

The BSDP involved an iterative learning approach, which often was adaptive and opportunistic. By providing this self assessment of the experience, we hope that the lessons can be shared, and that benefits can be realized by having paused, recorded, and reflected. Although the BSDP has officially concluded, the learning process continues as ideas are exchanged and contacts are continued.

ACKNOWLEDGEMENTS

The authors would like to thank our Indonesian and Canadian colleagues for their valuable contributions to the design of the study and the conduct of the field work. The financial support of the Canadian International Development Agency for the project is gratefully recognized, as well as the support of the University Consortium on the Environment, the organization within which the Bali Sustainable Development Project functioned, and the Environmental Management and Development Indonesia project.

REFERENCES

Ariani, A.A., & Kindon, S. (1995). Women, gender and sustainable development in Bali: In S. Martopo & B. Mitchell (Eds.), *Bali: balancing environment, economy and culture* (pp. 507-519). Department of Geography Publication Series No. 44. Waterloo: University of Waterloo.

Bali Sustainable Development Project. (1992). *Sustainable development strategy for Bali.* University Consortium on the Environment Research Paper No. 40. Yogyakarta, Java: Gadjah Mada University, and Waterloo, Ontario: University of Waterloo, in association with Udayana University, Bali.

Bali Sustainable Development Project. (1993). *Gender and development training workshop.* S. Kindon (Ed.), University Consortium on the Environment Research Paper No. 48. Yogyakarta, Java: Gadjah Mada University, and Waterloo, Ontario: University of Waterloo, in association with Udayana University, Bali.

Bankoff, G. (1993). *Changing perceptions of the environment, state and society in maritime southeast Asia.* Working Paper No. 14. Canberra: National Library of Australia.

Biswas, A.K. (1996). Capacity building for water management: some personal thoughts. *International Journal of Water Resources Development,* 12(4), 399-405.

Boehmer, K., Haight, M., &. Mitchell, B. (1997). *Guidelines for integrated watershed management training.* Jakarta: Indonesian Ministry of Education and Culture, Environmental Studies Development in Indonesia Project.

Catlett, M., & Schuftan, C. (1994). Lessons from institution building in Kenya. *Public Administration and Development,* 14 (2), 153-168.

Centre for Environmental Studies. (1995). *Community development of Code River basin: draft final report.* Yogyakarta: Gadjah Mada University, Centre for Environmental Studies.

Clark, B. (1987). EIA training for developing countries. *Strengthening environmental co-operation with developing countries* (pp. 117-128). Paris, Organization for Economic Co-operation and Development.

Cohen, J.M. (1992). Foreign advisors and capacity building: the case of Kenya. *Public Administration and Development,* 12 (5), 493-510.

Cohen, J.M. (1995). Capacity building in the public sector: a focused framework for analysis and action. *International Review of Administrative Sciences,* 61 (3), 407-422.

Cukier, J., Norris, J., & Wall, G. (1996). The involvement of women in the tourism of Bali, Indonesia. *Journal of Development Studies 33 (2),* 248-270.

Cummings, F.H. (1993). Project planning and administrative lessons from the Sulawesi Regional Development Project. *Canadian Journal of Development Studies Special Issue,* 137-166.

Currey, B. (1993). Environmental leadership training for Asia. *Development in Practice,* 3 (3), 196-203.

Eiseman, F.B. (1989a). *Bali: sekala and niskala volume I, essays on religion, ritual and art.* Berkeley-Singapore: Periplus Editions.

Eiseman, F.B. (1989b). *Bali: sekala and siskala volume II, essays on society, tradition and craft.* Berkeley-Singapore: Periplus Editions.

Gertler, L. (1993). One country, two concepts: variations on sustainability. *Canadian Journal of Development Studies Special Issue,* 103-122.

Gertler, L. (1995). The village of Seraya Tengah: a sustainable development perspective. In S. Martopo & B. Mitchell (Eds.), *Bali: balancing environment, economy and culture (pp. 389-410).* Department of Geography Publication Series No. 44. Waterloo: University of Waterloo.

Grindle, M.S., & Hilderbrand, M.E. (1995). Building sustainable capacity in the public sector: what can be done? *Public Administration and Development,* 15 (5), 441-463.

Gupta, A., & Hyma. B. (1995). "Towards gender-sensitive planning for achieving locally sustainable and effective use of community drinking and domestic water supply systems: a case study from Tengipis, Bali. In S. Martopo & B. Mitchell (Eds.), *Bali: balancing environment, economy and culture* (pp. 465-487). Department of Geography Publication Series No. 44. Waterloo: University of Waterloo.

Haight, M.E., & Ratha, M. (1995). Wastes: issues and opportunities. In S. Martopo & B. Mitchell (Eds.), *Bali: balancing environment, economy and culture (pp. 215-236).* Department of Geography Publication Series No. 44. Waterloo: University of Waterloo.

Hartvelt, F. (1996). Capacity building program for sustainable water sector development. *International Journal of Water Resources Development.* 12 (4), 407-411.

Hulme, D. (1989). Learning and not learning from experience in rural project planning. *Public Administration and Development.* 9 (1), 1-16.

Jensen, G.D., & Suryani, L.K. (1992). *The Balinese people: a reinvestigation of character.* Oxford: Oxford University Press.

Kidd, A.D. (1993). Analysis of an approach to developing "viable policy": a case study of a university linkage project. *Land Use Policy 10 (1),* 16-25.

Kiggundu, M. N. (1989). *Managing organizations in developing countries: an operational and strategic approach.* West Hartford, Connecticut: Kumarian Press.

Kluchhon, C. (1951). The study of culture. In D. Leiner and H.E.D. Laswell (Eds.), *The policy sciences* (pp. 78-107). Stanford: Stanford University Press.

Kusumandari, A., & Mitchell, B. (1997). Soil erosion and sediment yield in forest and agroforestry areas in West Java, Indonesia. *Journal of Soil and Water Conservation 52 (5),* 376-380.

Lee, K.N. (1993). *Compass and gyroscope: integrating science and politics for the environment.* Washington, DC: Island Press.

Mabbett, H. (1989). *The Balinese.* Wellington: New Zealand: January Books.

Martopo, S., & Mitchell, B. (Eds). (1995). *Bali: balancing environment, economy and culture.* Department of Geography Publication Series No. 44. Waterloo: University of Waterloo.

Martopo, S., & Mitchell, B. (1995). The capacity for village sustainability in Bali. *Manusia dan Lingkungan,* 2 (5), 14-33.

Mattingly, M. (1989). Implementing planning with teaching: using training to make it happen. *Third World Planning Review,* 11 (4), 417-428.

Mitchell, B. (1994a). Sustainable development at the village level in Bali, Indonesia. *Human Ecology,* 22 (2), 189-211.

Mitchell, B. (1994b). Institutional obstacles to sustainable development in Bali, Indonesia. *Singapore Journal of Tropical Geography,* 15 (2), 145-156.

Mitchell, B. (1995). Sustainable development strategy for Bali. In S. Martopo & B. Mitchell, (Eds), *Bali: balancing environment, economy and culture* (pp. 537-566). Department of Geography Publication Series No. 44. Waterloo: University of Waterloo, 537-566.

Nelson, J.G. (1991). Research in human ecology and planning: an interactive, adaptive approach. *Canadian Geographer,* 35 (2), 114-127.

Petrich, C.H. (1993). Indonesia and global climate change negotiations: potential opportunities and constraints for participation, leadership, and commitment. *Global Environmental Change,* 3 (1), 53-77.

Rendha, W. (1995). Foreword. In S. Martopo & B. Mitchell (Eds.), *Bali: balancing environment, economy and culture* (pp. v-viii). Department of Geography Publication Series No. 44. Waterloo: University of Waterloo.

Rondinelli, D.A. (1993a). *Development projects as policy experiments: an adaptive approach to development administration.* London: Routledge.

Rondinelli, D A. (1993b). *Strategic and results-based management.* Ottawa: Canadian International Development Agency.

Sloan, N.A., & Sugandhy. (1994). An overview of Indonesian coastal environmental management. *Coastal Management,* 22 (3), 215-233.

Stockman, R. (1997) The sustainability of development projects: an impact assessment of German vocational-training projects in Latin America. *World Development,* 25 (11), 1767-1784.

Telfer, D., and Wall, G. (1996) "Linkages between tourism and food production" *Annals of Tourism Research*, 23 (3), 635-653.

Timothy, D., & Wall, G. (1995). Tourist accommodation in an Asian city. *Journal of Tourism Studies*, 6 (2), 63-73.

Unesco. (1982). *The Mexico City declaration on cultural policies.* Mexico City: MONDIACULT.

University Consortium on the Environment. (1992). *Self-Evaluation.* Bandung: Institute of Technology, Yogyakarta: Gadjah Mada University; Jakarta: University of Indonesia; Waterloo: University of Waterloo; North York: York University.

Van Steenberg, F. (1992). Regional development and the planning framework: the case of Indonesia. *Tijschrift voor Economische en Sociale Geografie*, 83 (3), 216-225.

Vickers, A. (1989). *Bali: a paradise created.* Berkeley-Singapore: Periplus Editions, Inc.

Wall, G. (1993). International collaboration in the search for sustainable tourism in Bali, Indonesia. *Journal of Sustainable Tourist*, 1 (1), 38-47.

Wall, G. (1995a). Forces for change: tourism. In S. Martopo & B. Mitchell (Eds.), *Bali: balancing environment, economy and culture* (pp. 57-74). Department of Geography Publication Series No. 44. Waterloo: University of Waterloo, 57-74.

Wall, G. (1995b). *Introduction to ecotourism: training modules.* Environmental Studies Centres Development in Indonesia Project. Halifax: Dalhousie University, and Jakarta: Direktorat Jenderal Pendidikan Tinggi, Departemen Pendidikan dan Kebudayaan.

Wall, G. (1996). Perspectives on tourism in selected Balinese villages. *Annals of Tourism Research*, 23 (1), 123-137.

Weiskel, T.C. (1993). UNCED and after: global issues, country problems, and regional solutions in the Asia-Pacific area. *Journal of Developing Areas*, 28 (1), 13-20.

Welles, H. (1995). EIA capacity-strengthening in Asia: the USAID-WRI model. *Environmental Professional*, 17 (2), 103-116.

Wiggins, S. (1985). The planning and management of integrated rural development in drylands: early lessons from Kenya's arid and semi-arid lands programs. *Public Administration and Development*, 5 (2), 91-108.

Women's Study Centre. (1995). *The role of women and men in environmental health in rural and urban areas of the Code River basin, Yogyakarta.* Yogyakarta: Gadjah Mada University, Women's Study Centre.

Women's Study Centre, Centre for Environmental Studies, Centre for Tourism Studies, Tourism Research Development Association, & University Consortium on the Environment. (1995). *Proceedings: national symposium, gender and tourism development.* Yogyakarta: Gadjah Mada University, Women's Study Centre.

Interfirm Channel Relationships, Influence Strategies and Performance in China: An Empirical Examination

Hong Liu
Yen Po Wang

SUMMARY. This paper empirically examines the relationship between inter-firm channel relationships, influence strategies and suppliers' performance. A survey of 103 foreign partners from Sino-foreign joint ventures in the food industry in China shows that channel relationships have a major positive effect on supplier's channel performance. While the influence strategy of "threats" is negatively related to supplier's channel performance and channel relationships, "suggestive litigation" has a positive influence on performance, on the contrary to findings in Western countries. Although a business relationship with an emphasis on "legal effect" is not desired on the part of distributors, it enhances channel relationships. The influence strategy of "request" as a Western phenomenon does not work well in China, and has an inverse effect on channel relationships. Implications for practitioners and researchers are discussed. *[Article copies available for a fee from The Haworth Document Delivery Service: 1-800-342-9678. E-mail address: getinfo@haworthpressinc.com <Website: http://www.haworthpressinc.com>]*

Hong Liu is Lecturer in Marketing and Director, China Business Centre, Manchester Business School, Booth Street West, Manchester M15 6PB, England (E-mail: h.liu@fs2.mbs.ac.uk).

Yen Po Wang is a Doctoral Candidate at Manchester Business School, England.

[Haworth co-indexing entry note]: "Interfirm Channel Relationships, Influence Strategies and Performance in China: An Empirical Examination." Liu, Hong, and Yen Po Wang. Co-published simultaneously in *Journal of Transnational Management Development* (International Business Press, an imprint of The Haworth Press, Inc.) Vol. 4, No. 3/4, 1999, pp. 135-152; and: *Culture and International Business* (ed: Kip Becker) International Business Press, an imprint of The Haworth Press, Inc., 2000, pp. 135-152. Single or multiple copies of this article are available for a fee from The Haworth Document Delivery Service [1-800-342-9678, 9:00 a.m. - 5:00 p.m. (EST). E-mail address: getinfo@haworthpressinc.com].

135

KEYWORDS. Distribution channel, relationship, influence strategies, performance, China

INTRODUCTION

The fastest growing economy in the world over the past fifteen years, China has recently been ranked by the World Bank as the seventh largest economy calculated based on the three-years adjusted exchange rate method. It will have 230 million middle-income consumers and a retail market potentially worth more than $900 billion by 2005 (Chan, Perez, Perkins, & Shu, 1997). As more and more foreign companies woo consumer market shares in China, distribution is increasingly becoming a major stumbling block (Byrne, Woodard & Chow, 1994) as well as a key success factor for their operations. Coca-Cola has hitherto outperformed its arch-rival PepsiCo in China largely due to its effective distribution strategy. Despite a late start in China, Goodyear Tire and Rubber has become a key foreign player in the country's tire market. Its success has, to a large extent, been ascribed to its commitment to developing effective distribution channels.

Although there has been substantial research on behavioral aspects of distribution channel in the USA (Lusch & Brown, 1996; Frazier & Rody, 1991) and European countries (Hakansson & Johanson, 1988; Hallen, Johanson & Seyed-Mohammed, 1991), and some studies on distribution channels within developing countries such as Saudi Arabia (Al-Motawa & Ahmed, 1996) and India (Frazier, Gill & Kale, 1989; Kale, 1986), inadequate attention has been paid to dyadic interactions in international settings (Chan, 1991; Rosenbloom & Larsen, 1991; Sakano, Cote & Onzo, 1993; Shoham, Rose & Kropp, 1997). In their research of relationships between foreign manufacturers and their distributors in Saudi Arabia, Al-Motawa and Ahmed (1996, p. 50) found that the pattern of relationship in Saudi Arabia was not consistent with the general findings based on studies in industrialized countries in the literature.

It has been recognized that successful operations in China need to follow a different marketing paradigm: relational–conflict–neo-classic, compared with the typical one in Western developed countries: neo-classic–conflict-relational (Ambler, 1994). If channel relationship has a major effect on channel member performance in Western countries (Beckett-Camarata, Camarata & Barker, 1998), it would be even more so in China. Guanxi[1] (connection)-style buyer-seller relationships similar to relationship marketing were found to be strongly related to reduced levels of perceived uncertainty about the business environment and a variety of improved performance outcomes (Abramson & Ali, 1997). Findings from a recent empirical study suggest that guanxi-based business variables has a significant and positive effect on joint ventures' accounting and market performance (Luo, 1997). Unfortunately, studies on channel relationship management in China have been far few and between.

This study empirically examines the patterns of guanxi-style channel relationships between foreign funded enterprises (FFEs) and their independent distributors and the influence strategies used by FFEs to achieve distributors' cooperation or support and the effect of such relationships and influence strategies on FFEs' channel performance in China. More specifically, the following questions are addressed:

1. What is the structure/pattern of channel relationships between FFEs and independent distributors in China and how do such relationships influence the company's performance?
2. What are influence strategies used by foreign partners to secure distributors' co-operation, and how successful do these strategies enhance the company's performance?
3. How do influence strategies affect guanxi-style channel relationships?

The paper reviews the literature on channel relationships and develops a influence strategy-relationship-performance model. Then, research methodology used in the study is described, followed by a presentation and discussion of survey results in the food sector in China. Finally, conclusions and limitations are drawn and implications for both researchers and practitioners are discussed.

LITERATURE REVIEW

The behavioral approach to the study of interactions between channel members provides a foundation for the concept of relationship management (Rosson & Ford, 1982; Rosenbloom, 1990). Behavioral researchers support the proposition that the better management and coordination of behavioral interactions in channels dyads would enhance channel members' performance and lead to sustainable competitive advantage in the market place (Weitz & Wensley, 1988; Beckett-Camarata, Camarata & Barker, 1998).

Commitment has been seen as an important dimension in building and maintaining channel relationships (Mayo, 1993; Mohr & Nevin, 1990). Commitment can have several facets, but there are two that are most relevant to channel exchange relationships: *continuant* (or *calculative*) and *affective* (or *attitudinal*) (Johnson & Raven, 1996; Allen & Meyer, 1990). A channel participant's commitment to the channel relationship pivots on (among other things) their perceptions of their partner's commitment (Anderson & Weitz, 1992; Sriram & Mummalaneni, 1990). It has been found that the longer the relationship lasts, the stronger are the bounds of trust and commitment between the two collaborative parties (Sriram & Mummalaneni, 1990).

Another dimension of channel relationship is trust. In a marketing exchange relationship, trust is defined as "the firm's belief that another company will perform actions that will result in positive outcomes for the firm, as well as not taking unexpected actions that would result in negative outcomes for the firm" (Anderson & Narus, 1990). Thus, development and maintenance of trust is essential for a productive long-term channel relationship. Johnson and Raven (1996) found that self reports of high quality relationship are associated with self reports of enhanced outcomes in terms of satisfaction and performance.

Influence strategies "involve the alternative means of communication available to a firm's personnel in their influence attempts with associated channel members" (Frazier & Rody, 1991). Two types of influence strategies have been identified: (1) *strategies based on altering perceptions:* information exchange and recommendations and (2) *strategies not based on perceptual change:* promises, threats, legalistic pleas, and requests (Frazier & Summers, 1984). Empirical studies have shown the use of coercive power (promise, threat, and legalistic pleas) are negatively related to relationships and performance. Tables 1 and 2 summarize the results of previous empirical studies concerning relationships between power, channel relationships and performance.

RESEARCH FRAMEWORK AND PROPOSITIONS

Figure 1 presents the research model, which is based on the literature review and some interviews undertaken by authors in China. As

TABLE 1. Summary Results of Studies in Distribution Channel Relationship

Other Relational	Power Source Constructs	Manufacturer's Use of Influence Strategies	
		Non-Coercive	**Coercive**
Channel Relationship	**Continuant Commitment**	+ (c)	
	Affective Commitment	+ (c)	
	Co-Operation	n.r. (g)	
Relational Outcomes	**Performance (subjective)**	+ (f.e)	− (f.e)
	Satisfaction	+ (b,d,c)	− (a,b)

Note: 1. "+" = positive relationship; "−" = inverse relationship

2. Letters in parentheses refer to grounds for each relationship:

a: Frazier, Gill and Kale (1989)
b: Frazier and Summers (1986)
c: Pan and Du (1993)
d: Al-Motawa and Ahmed (1996)
e: Gaski (1986)
f: Boyle and Dwyer (1995)
g: Johnson, Sakano and Onzo (1990)

TABLE 2. Summary Results of Studies in Distribution Channel Relationship

Outcomes vs. Relationship		Relational Outcomes	
		Performance	**Satisfaction**
Interchannel Relationship	**Continuant Commitment**	+ (h,i)	+ (h,i)
	Affective Commitment	+ (h,i)	+ (h,i)
	Trust	+ (h, j)	+ (h, j)

Note: 1. "+" = positive relationship; "−" = inverse relationship; "n.r." = no significant relationship

2. Letters in parentheses refer to grounds for each relationship:

h: Mayo (1993)
j: Aniderson and Narus (1990)
i: Meyer and Allen (1984)

shown in the model, channel relationship is positively related to performance (Mayo, 1993; Meyer & Allen, 1984). Thus, we propose that in China:

H1: The better the guanxi-based channel relationships are, the better the performance; alternatively, an adversarial relationship results in worse performance.

FIGURE 1. A Model of Channel Relationships and Performance in China

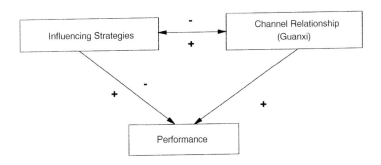

Table 1 indicates that empirical studies in Western economies suggest that non-coercive related power be positively associated with channel relationships (Pan & Du, 1993) and performance (Boyle & Dwyer, 1995; Gaski 1982; Frazier & Summers, 1986; Al-Motawa & Ahmed, 1996; Pan & Du, 1993), while coercive related power be negatively related to channel relationships (Pan & Du, 1993) and performance (Boyle & Dwyer, 1995; Gaski, 1982; Frazier, Gill & Kale, 1989).

Therefore, influence strategies can be positively and negatively related with channel relationships and performance, depending on the type of strategies to be used. In this study, we hypothesize that in China:

H2A: Non-coercive type of influence strategies tends to be positively associated with guanxi-based channel relationships.

H2B: Coercive type of influence strategies tends to be negatively related to guanxi-based channel relationships.

H3A: Non-coercive type of influence strategies tends to be positively correlated with performance.

H3B: Coercive type of strategies tends to be negatively related to performance.

Proactive and incentive type of strategies generally nurtures and cultivates as well as reflects good relationships, and thus is positively associated with performance. In contrast, reactive and penalizing type of strategies often reflects unsatisfactory or poor performance and a troubled relationship taking place, which require some "reactive" strategies to remedy it.

RESEARCH METHODOLOGY

Research Procedure

There are two stages in this study. In Stage 1, pilot interviews were conducted in both England and China to examine the applicability of some constructs identified in the literature and test the questionnaire. In Stage 2, a postal survey was undertaken in China to test hypotheses.

Since the target audience was foreign suppliers in China, the questionnaire was designed in English. It was tested with 41 informants in relevant key positions, and amended accordingly. A systematic discriminating sampling was carried out. The discriminating criteria included (1) the company's form of investment was either a joint venture or a wholly-owned subsidiary; (2) the company was operating in the consumer food industry; (3) the company had manufacturing operations in China; (4) the company was inward selling a large proportion of its China production; (5) the company employed local third-party distributors in their channel arrangements; and (6) the company had been in local operation for at least one year.

The procedure of the sampling included obtaining inclusive lists of foreign investments in Beijing, Tianjin, Shanghai, Hangzhou, Guangzhou and Shenzhen from each regional Bureau of Foreign direct Investment. After critically screening the lists, 684 qualified foreign-funded companies were identified. The circulation of questionnaire was helped by the China's National Food Association.

The questionnaires were sent to 684 companies, with a cover letter from the China's National Food Association. Two weeks later, the companies were reminded of the survey by telephone, fax or personal visits. One month after the first reminder, second copies of the questionnaire, together with a reminding letter, were either posted, faxed or delivered personally to the respondents who had not replied to the questionnaires. Follow-up efforts were made two weeks after the second wave of the questionnaire. The questionnaire distribution and follow up were repeated for the third time one month after the second follow up.

A total of 121 questionnaires were returned or collected. Of these questionnaires, 18 of them were either not answered properly (i.e., too many unanswered questions) or failed to satisfy the confirmatory mechanisms, and hence discarded, with 103 useable questionnaires (a response rate of 15.06%). A data checking procedure was followed, and no systematic bias was identified.

Factor analysis was performed, with principal components as the extraction method and varimax as the rotation method, to "generate" or confirm *a priori* conceptualization of constructs. Multiple regression analyses were subsequently performed to test the propositions.

Measurement

The variables measuring relationship, influence strategy, and performance were factor analyzed to generate operational constructs. The choice of these variables was based on the literature and in-depth interviews conducted in China. The results of factor analysis of different measures are discussed as follows.

Performance. Nine variables were included to measure performance. The factor analysis of these measures has generated two factors: *Financial (Performance) Index* and *Operational (Performance) Index*. The results of the factor analysis are displayed in Table 3. As can be seen, the Cronbach alphas were 0.7808 and 0.7317 for *Finan-*

TABLE 3. The Results of Factor Analysis of Performance Measures

Factor	Variables	Loadings	Alpha
Financial Index	Return on investment	0.891	
	Net profit margin	0.853	
	Overall financial accomplishment	0.564	
	Inventory level	0.557	0.7808
Operational Index	Market covered	0.882	
	Geographical coverage	0.862	
	Satisfaction with distributor's performance	0.550	
	Product/service quality	0.472	
	Sales goals	0.460	0.7317

NB: Only loading values greater than 0.45 are reported and interpreted.

cial Index and *Operational Index* respectively, indicating a high level of internal consistency and reliability.

Channel Relationship (Guanxi). Factor analysis of the nineteen variables measuring channel relationship yield four factors, which can be labelled *Trust-Commitment, Harmonious Relationship, Affective Relationship* and *Adversary Relationship* in a descending order (from better to worse), as shown in Table 4. Cronbach alphas for each factor were 0.9812, 0.7507, 0.7498 and 0.6773 respectively. In addition, *Trust-Commitment, Harmonious Relationship,* and *Adversary Relationship* may be seen as the relationship type of "Calculative Commitment" (vs. Affective Commitment) (Johnson and Raven, 1996; Allen & Meyer, 1990).

Influence Strategies. Variables measuring influence strategies were factor analyzed, and four factors emerged, with adequate Cronbach alphas of 0.9812, 0.7507, 0.7498, and 0.6773, as displayed in Table 5.

TABLE 4. The Results of Factor Analysis of Relationship Measures

Factor	Variables	Loadings	Alpha
Trust-Commitment	Keep promises	0.781	
	Sharing problems and communications	0.756	
	Dependency on distributor	0.752	
	Belief in distributor's truthfulness	0.713	
	Importance of good relationship	0.605	
	Distributor's commitment to performance	0.559	0.8189
Harmonious Relationship	Importance of "guanxi"	0.743	
	Understanding of "guanxi" and "face"	0.734	
	Business relationship	0.689	
	Continued relationship/commitment	0.675	
	Joint decisions	0.653	
	Importance of "preserving face"	0.634	
	Co-operative relationship	0.508	0.8524
Adversary Relationship	Full of conflict	0.870	
	Full of tension and disagreement	0.812	
	Frustrating and hostile	0.804	0.9035
Affective Relationship	Desire/willingness for good relationship	0.770	
	Emotional attachment	0.675	
	Driven by human relationship	0.594	0.6162

NB: Only loading values greater than 0.45 are reported and interpreted.

TABLE 5. Influence Strategy Constructs

Factor	Variables	Loadings	Alpha
Suggestive	Implying non-compliance consequence	0.975	
Litigation	Referring to legal agreement	0.963	
	Suggesting the agreement implication	0.959	0.9812
Rewards	Benefits from following recommendations	0.798	
	Make more money by following suggestions	0.727	
	Receive better services by following suggestions	0.659	
	Incentives for joint promotions	0.650	
	Suggestions mean to help	0.615	0.7507
Threats	Threats of such as higher prices and slower delivery	0.831	
	Will result in penalties if not complying requests	0.765	
	Suggest poor services if not complying requests	0.711	0.7498
Request	Demand compliance without incentives/enforcement	0.721	
	Pushing new ideas without explanations	0.686	
	Promise to give them something if they comply	0.650	0.6773

NB: Only loading values greater than 0.45 are reported and interpreted.

According to the loading variables, these factors can be named as *Suggestive Litigation, Rewards, Threats,* and *Request.*

RESULTS AND DISCUSSION

Company Profiles

Table 6 shows the profiles of sample companies. As can be seen from Table 6a, about 57% of respondents were either general managers/managing directors or territory managers/directors. The rest were directors or managers affiliated with the marketing department ("Others" include 2 "Distribution Managers" and 1 "Marketing Consultant"). In addition, none of the working relationships between the company and its primary distributor were active for less than a year, and about 57% of the sample companies employed the distributors for more than 4 years. The working relationships in the sample companies were relatively shorter compared with those in Western countries. This is largely because China did not open its door until the early 1980s,

TABLE 6a. Company Profiles

	Number	%
Position of Respondents		
Managing Director/General Manager	20	19.4
Territory Director/Manager	39	37.9
Marketing Director/Manager	22	21.4
Sales Director/Manager	19	18.4
Others	3	2.9
Company's Years of Working Relationship with the Primary Distributor		
1-3 years	42	42.9
4-6 years	49	50.0
7-9 years	5	5.1
More than 10 years	2	2.0
Unanswered	5	Missing

TABLE 6b. Company Profiles

Company's Country of Origin	Number	%
United Kingdom	17	17.0
United States	14	14.0
Continental Europe	20	20.0
Japan	10	10.0
Taiwan	17	17.0
HongKong/Macao	11	11.0
South East Asia	7	7.0
Others	4	4.0
Unanswered	3	Missing

TABLE 6c. Company Profiles

	Number	%
Entry Method		
Equity Joint Venture	70	68.6
Contractual/Co-operative Joint Venture	6	5.9
Wholly-Owned Foreign Subsidiary	26	25.5
Unanswered	1	Missing
% of Equity Owned by the Respondent's Company*		
1-25%	5	7.1
26-50%	21	30.0
51-75%	32	45.7
76-99%	12	17.2

*Only applicable to companies involving equity joint ventures

and a large proportion of foreign direct investment went into China in the early 1990s. This is one of the special features of this study.

As displayed in Table 6b, sixty-one percent of the sample companies were direct investment from the USA, Europe and Japan, with the remaining companies from Taiwan, Hong Kong/Macao, and other South East Asian countries. Table 6c indicates that about 75% of the sample companies took the form of joint ventures (either equity, contractual, or cooperative), while about 25% used the form of wholly foreign-owned enterprises. Joint ventures have often been encouraged by the Chinese government and given preferential treatment such as tax holidays and inward selling rights, and they appear to be more appropriate for firms that have first gone into China without prior experience. In addition, until recently, the form of wholly-foreign-owned companies has not been granted for many sectors including the food.

It is notable from Table 6c that about 63% of the sample companies reported owning the majority share of joint ventures. This reflects the recent trend in China that foreign investors in China have sought to maintain the control of joint venture operations.

Hypothesis Testing

The results of regression analysis in Table 7 suggest that Proposition H1 is supported, that is, the better the channel relationships are, the better the performance is; alternatively, an adversary relationship results in worse performance. As shown in the table, *Trust-Commit-*

TABLE 7. Multiple Regression Analysis of Relationship and Performance Constructs

Dependent Variable	Standardised Regression Coefficients						
	FTC	FHR	FAR	FER	F	Sig F	Adjusted R^2
FFI	0.302***	0.165	− 0.250**	0.076	5.615	0.000	0.153
FOI	0.529***	0.170*	− 0.193*	0.022	13.023	0.000	0.320

NB: Significance level is represented by: *$p < 0.05$; **$p < 0.01$; ***$p < 0.001$

FFI: Financial Index	FHR: Harmonious Relationship
FOI: Operational Index	FAR: Adversary Relationship
FTC: Trust-Commitment	FER: Affective Relationship

ment is a major determinant of both *Financial Index* and *Operational Index* ($B_{ffi\text{-}ftc}$ = 0.302, p < 0.001; $B_{foi\text{-}ftc}$ = 0.529, p < 0.001), and *Adversary Relationship* has a negative effect on both *Financial Index* and *Operational Index* ($B_{ffi\text{-}far}$ = −0.250, p < 0.01; $B_{foi\text{-}far}$ = −0.193, p < 0.05). It is noticeable that *Harmonious Relationship* was marginally correlated with *Financial Index* (p < 0.1) and significantly with *Operational Index* (p < 0.05). The confirmation of the hypothesis also verifies the traditional notion that guanxi is a key success factor for doing business in China.

Table 8 displays the results of multiple regression analysis of influence strategies and relationship constructs. As seen in the table, Propositions H2A and H2B are partially supported. *Request,* a non-coercive strategy, has a negative effect on *Trust-Commitment,* and this relationship is contrary to that found in Western countries (Pan & Du, 1993) and proposition H2A. *Trust-Commitment* is an important reflection of guanxi at its best between the two parties. Building up guanxi involves reciprocal favors or benefits. *Request* is largely a Western "business concept" and a way of business dealing, and does not work well in China.

As displayed in Table 8, *Harmonious Relationship* is positively influenced by *Suggestive Litigation* (this rejects Proposition H2B) and negatively and strongly affected by *Threats* (this supports Proposition H2B). In addition, *Request* also has a negative effect on *Harmonious*

TABLE 8. Multiple Regression Analysis of Influence Strategy and Relationship Constructs

Dependent Variable	Standardised Regression Coefficients						
	FSL	FR	FT	FD	F	Sig F	Adjusted R^2
FTC	0.174	0.102	−0.039	−0.312**	3.981	0.005	0.140
FHR	0.212**	0.060	−0.542***	−0.176*	14.614	0.000	0.348
FAR	0.064	0.097	0.213*	0.162	2.275	0.067	0.048
FER	−0.488***	0.093	0.089	0.083	8.669	0.000	0.231

NB: Significance level is represented by: *p < 0.05; **p < 0.01; ***p < 0.001

FTC: Trust-Commitment
FHR: Harmonious Relationship
FAR: Adversary Relationship
FER: Affective Relationship

FSL: Suggestive Litigation
FR: Rewards
FT: Threats
FD: Request

Relationship, similar to its influence *on Trust-Commitment.* An explanation for the positive relationship of *Harmonious Relationship* with *Suggestive Litigation* is similar to that with *Performance.* That is, *Suggestive Litigation* serves as the definition of the distributor's behavior within an acceptable or satisfactory boundary, resulting in a harmonious relationship. It is particularly noteworthy that *Suggestive Litigation* has a negative effect on *Affective Relationship* ($B_{fsl-fer}$ = -0.488, p < 0.001), indicating that *Suggestive Litigation* is not desirable on the part of distributors but actually plays an important role in maintaining a healthy supplier-distributor relationship.

Table 9 indicates that proposition H3B is supported, while proposition H3A is rejected. As shown in the table, the influence strategy of *Threats* has a negative influence on performance, and this is consistent with research findings in Western economies (Royle & Dwyer, 1995; Gaski, 1982). Interestingly, *Rewards* as a kind of non-coercive influence strategy are negatively associated with *Operational Index,* contrary to findings in Western economies (Royle & Dwyer, 1995; Gaski, 1982). (B_{foi-fr} = -0.197; p < 0.05). This result may be due to the fact that, when performance in the company deteriorated, the strategy of *Rewards* was used to motivate the distributor.

In addition, *Suggestive Litigation* was found to be significantly and positively related to performance. In contrast, studies in Western economies suggest a negative relationship between legalistic pleas and performance (Frazier, Gill & Kale, 1989; Frazier & Summers, 1986). *Suggestive Litigation* may be seen as an indication of "business relationship." As pilot case studies in China have suggested, a business

TABLE 9. Multiple Regression Analysis of Performance and Influence Strategy Constructs

Dependent Variable	Standardised Regression Coefficients						
	FSL	FR	FT	FD	F	Sig F	Adjusted R^2
FFI	−0.145	−0.008	−0.240*	−0.122	2.523	0.046	0.056
FOI	0.236***	−0.197*	−0.228*	−0.097	4.536	0.002	0.122

NB: Significance level is represented by: *p < 0.05; **p < 0.01; ***p < 0.001

FFI: Financial Index   FR: Rewards
FOI: Operational Index   FT: Threats
FSL: Suggestive Litigation   FD: Request

relationship plus a good personal relationship tend to result in better performance, while a pure personal based relationship without a business relationship (formal contract) tends to bring about worse performance. A suggestive litigation strategy would define a distributor's behavior within the boundary of contract, without actually utilizing legalistic pleas to penalize the distributor. In this way, more often than not, a good personal relationship can be maintained (it is notable that *Suggestive Litigation* is positively correlated with *Harmonious Relationship,* as shown in Table 8). In China, the concept of "legality" or "law" has been extremely weak because of the long-standing absence of law, the traditions of emphasizing personal relationships/guanxi and the "Cultural Revolution" when unlawful behavior dominated.

CONCLUSIONS

As China is increasingly becoming one of the largest consumer markets in the world, overcoming distribution barriers and increasing channel efficiency and coverage are at the top of the agenda for many foreign firms operating in China. Despite a substantial body of research on channel relationships in Western economies, studies on channel relationships in China have been extremely limited. In particular, considering that "relationship" has been widely accepted to be a major factor influencing success or failure, it is imperative and significant to understand the structure and influences of channel relationships in China.

This is one of the few studies that has empirically examined the relationship between channel relationships, influence strategies and suppliers' performance in China. A survey of 103 foreign funded enterprises in China has identified different relationship patterns between channel relationships, influence strategies and performance from those in Western countries. The major differences and their implications for practitioners and researchers are presented as follows.

The best supplier-distributor relationship (guanxi) in China is reflected in suppliers' trust and commitment to their distributors. Channel relationships are a major determinant of a supplier's performance: the better the relationship, the better the performance. An adversary relationship has a major negative effect on a supplier's performance. Therefore, to achieve business success in China it is important to

nurture and invest in building up relationships with Chinese distributors.

Having a business relationship through emphasizing or reminding
the legal effect of the contract is important in China, where legal
concepts and instruments have largely been absent in the past. The
influence strategy of *Threats* negatively affects channel relationships
and results in worse supplier's performance. Thus, such a coercive
type of strategy should be avoided whenever possible. Although a
supplier-distributor relationship with a repeated reminding of legal
effect is not desired on part of distributors, its positive influences and
benefits dominate. The influence strategy of *Request* traditionally used
by Western firms does not work well in China.

Since the influence strategy construct in this study was largely
based on the concepts and findings in Western countries, future research is needed to identify constructs that better fit a Chinese context
and to understand better what factors bring about better or worse
supplier-distributor relationships.

The response rate was not as high as one might have expected.
However, given the general extreme difficulties in getting data from
foreign funded enterprises in China and the high quality responses
(country distribution, knowledge about distributors, and senior respondents), the response rate of 15% may be considered as acceptable
or satisfactory.

NOTE

1. Guanxi is a Chinese word which literally means *connection* or *networking,* and
it involves reciprocal obligations and favors between two parties in personal or business relations.

REFERENCES

Abramson, N.R. & Al, J. (1997). Using guanxi-style buyer-seller relationships in
China: Reducing uncertainty and improving performance outcome. *International
Executive,* 39 (6), 765-804.
Al-Motawa, A. & Ahmed, A. (1996). Control, Conflict and Satisfaction in Interna-
tional Channels: Autos in a Middle-Eastern Market. *Journal of Marketing Chan-
nels,* 5 (3/4), 49-69.
Allen, N. & Meyer, J. (1990). The Measurement and Antecedents of Affective,
Continuance and Normative Commitment to the Organization. *Journal of Occu-
pational Psychology,* 63, 1-18.

Ambler, T. (1994). Marketing's third paradigm: Guanxi. *Business Strategy Review,* 5 (Winter), 69-81.

Anderson, J. & Narus, J. (1990). A Model of Distributor Firm and Manufacturer Firm Working Partnerships. *Journal of Marketing,* 54, 42-58.

Anderson, E. & Weitz, B. (1992). The Use of Pledges to Build and Sustain Commitment in Distribution Channels. *Journal of Marketing Research,* 29, 18-34.

Beckett-Camarata, E.J., Camarata, M.R. & Barker, R.T. (1998). Integrating internal and external customer relationships through relationship management: A strategic response to a changing global environment. *Journal of Business Research,* 41 (1), 71-81.

Boyle, F. & Dwyer, F. (1995). Power, Bureaucracy, Influence and Performance: Their Relationships in Industrial Distribution Channels. *Journal of Business Research,* 32, 189-200.

Byrne, P.M., Woodard, K. & Chow, J. (1994). Success in China takes patience. *Transportation & Distribution,* 35, 53-56.

Chan, T.S. (1991). Export expansion process for electronics: a study of channel integration strategy. *Journal of Global Marketing,* 4 (4), 55-68.

Chan, W.W., Perez, J., Perkins, A., & Shu, M. (1997). China's retail markets are evolving more quickly than companies anticipate. *The McKingsey Quarterly,* 2, 206-211.

Frazier, G.L., Gill, J. & Kale, S. (1989). Dealer Dependence Levels and Reciprocal Actions in a Channel of Distribution in a Developing Country. *Journal of Marketing,* 53, 50-69.

Frazier, G.L. & Rody, C.R. (1991). The Use of Influence Strategies in Interfirm Relationships in Industrial Product Channels. *Journal of Marketing,* 55 (1), 52-69.

Frazier, G.L. & Summer, J.O. (1984). Interfirm Influence Strategies and Their Application Within Distribution Channels. *Journal of Marketing,* 48, 43-55.

Frazier, G. & Summers, J.O. (1986). Perceptions of inter-firm power and its use within a franchise channel of distribution. *Journal of Marketing Research,* 23, 169-76.

Gaski, J.F. (1986). Interrelations Among a Channel Entity's Power Sources: Impact of the Exercise of Reward and Coercion on Expert, Referent, and Legitimate Power Sources. *Journal of Marketing Research,* 23, 62-77.

Hakansson, H. & Johanson, J. (1988). Formal and Informal Co-Operation Strategies in International Industrial Networks. In F.J. Contractor & P. Lorange (Ed.), *Co-Operative Strategies in International Business* (pp. 369-379). Lexington, MA: Lexington Books.

Hallen, L., Johanson, J. & Seyed-Mohammed, N. (1991). Interfirm Adaptation in Business Relationships. *Journal of Marketing,* 55 (2), 29-38.

Johnson, J. & Raven, P. (1996). Relationship Quality, Satisfaction and Performance in Export Marketing Channels. *Journal of Marketing Channels,* 5 (3/4), 19-48.

Johnson, J.L., Sakano, T. & Onzo, N. (1990). Behavioral relations in a cross-culture distribution system: influence, control and conflict in US-Japanese marketing channels. *Journal of International Business Studies,* 21 (4), 639-655.

Kale, S.H. (1986). Dealer perceptions of manufacturing power and influence strategies in a developing country. *Journal of Marketing Research,* 23, 387-93.

Luo, Y. (1997). Guanxi and Performance of Foreign-invested Enterprises in China: An Empirical Inquiry. *Management International Review,* 37, 51-70.

Lusch, R. & Brown, J. (1996). Interdependency, Contracting, and Relational Behavior in Marketing Channels. *Journal of Marketing,* 60 (4), 19-39.

Mayo, D.T. (1993). Exchange Characteristics, Influence Strategies and Behavioral Outcomes in Channel Relationships: An Empirical Investigation. PhD Thesis: University of Alabama.

Meyer, J.P. & Allen, N. (1984). Testing the 'side-bet' theory of organizational commitment: some methodological considerations. *Journal of Applied Psychology,* 69, 372-378

Mohr, J. & Nevin, J.R. (1990). Communication Strategies in Marketing Channels: A Theoretical Perspective. *Journal of Marketing,* 54, 36-51.

Pan, M.C. & Du, Y.S. (1993). The interrelationships of inter-firm influence strategies with dependence, intrachannel conflict, and dealer satisfaction-an empirical study of the PC industry. *Tatung Journal,* 23, 142-64.

Rosenbloom, B. (1990). Motivating your international channel partners. *Business Horizons,* 33 (2), 53-57.

Rosenbloom, B. & Larsen, T. (1991). International channels of distribution and the role of comparative marketing analysis. *Journal of Global Marketing,* 4 (4), 39-54.

Rosson, P. & Ford, J.D. (1982). Manufacturer-overseas distributor relations and export performance. *Journal of International Business Studies,* (Fall), 57-72.

Sakano, Tomoaki, Cote, J.A., & Onzo, N. (1993), "The exercise of interfirm power and its repercussions in U.S.-Japanese channel relationships," *Journal of Marketing,* April, Vol. 57, 1-10.

Shoham, A., Rose, G.M., & Kropp, F. (1997). Conflict in International Channels of distribution. *Journal of Global Marketing,* 11 (2), 5-22.

Sriram, V. & Mummalaneni, V. (1990). Determinants of Source Loyalty in Buyer-Seller Relationships. *Journal of Purchasing and Materials Management,* 26 (4), 21-26.

Weitz, B.A. & Wensley, R. (1988). *Readings in Strategic Marketing: Analysis, Planning and Implementation.* Hinsdale, IL: The Dryden Press.

Index

[*Note:* Page numbers followed by f indicate figures; page numbers followed by t indicate tables.]

153

aspects of, 113-128
context of, 111-113
Environmental Management
    Development in Indonesia
    (EMDI) project, 110, 112-113
Ethical value systems, universal, 14,
    16-17
European Union (EU), 4
Expatriate(s)
    assignments of, financial expenses
        related to, 26
    failure rate of
        criteria in, 26
        in U.S. vs. Europe and Asia, 26
    social environment of
        patriates role in, networks in,
            27-38. *See also* Network(s),
            in patriate-expatriate
            experience
        patriates role in, 25-44
Expatriate managers, prominent, 31f

Farh, J-L, 45
Financial (Performance) Index,
    142-143,142t,147
Financial Times, 68-70
Foreign corporations, 13
Foreign direct investments (FDI), 6
Foreign funded enterprises (FFEs), in
    China, 137
Friedman, M., 10
Friesen, P.H., 91

Gender
    in BSDP, 125-126
    effect on managerial preference as
        measured by defender-
        prospector continuum, 88f,89
Gertler, L., 107,121
Ghemewat, P., 68-69
Ghoshal, S., 78
Glick, W.H., 86
Global business environment,
    changing profile of, 7-12

Global corporations, 12-13
Govindarajan, V., 91
Grindle, M.S., 108-110,129-130
Guanxi, 50
Guanxi (connection)-style buyer-seller
    relationships, in China, 137
Gudykunst, W.B., 2
Guthrie, J.P., 86,93

Hambrick, D.C., 87,93
Hamel, G., 76
Harmonious relationship, as factor in
    interfirm channel relationships,
    influence strategies, and
    performance in China, 143,
    143t
Harrigan, K.R., 75
Harrison, J.R., 11
Haryadi, 107
Hay, D., 51
Hennart, J.F., 75
Hergert, M., 68-69
Hilderbrand, M.E., 108-110,129-130
Hisrich, R.D., 99
Hofstede, G., 7-8,39,76
Horton, V., 67,69
Hulme, D., 130
Human resource issues, international,
    patriates role in, 38-42. *See
    also* Patriate(s), role in
    international human resource
    functions
Human resource management
    in China, township and village
        enterprises vs. Sino-foreign
        joint ventures, 45-65. *See
        also* China, human resources
        management practices in,
    institutional theory's link with, 48-49

Individual expatriate-individual
    patriate connection, 32-35
Individual-group connection, in
    patriate-expatriate
    experience, 29-32,31f,32f